# THE NEW
# RIDE WITH YOUR MIND
# CLINIC

# THE NEW
# RIDE WITH YOUR MIND
# CLINIC

### Rider biomechanics – basics to brilliance

## MARY WANLESS

TRAFALGAR SQUARE
North Pomfret, Vermont

First published in the United States of America in 2008 by
Trafalgar Square Books, North Pomfret, Vermont 05053

**Printed in China**

ISBN: 978-1-57076-391-5

Library of Congress Control Number: 2007908582

**Disclaimer of Liability**
The author and publisher shall have neither liability nor responsibility to any person or entity with
respect to any loss or damage caused or alleged to be caused directly or indirectly by the information
contained in this book. While the book is as accurate as the author can make it, there may be errors,
omissions, and inaccuracies.

Illustrations by Dianne Breeze (40, 54, 62, 74, 87, 90, 97, 101, 104 (bottom), 106, 116, 118, 119, 122,
130, 134, 168, 180), Christine Bousfield (78, 104 top, 158), and Peter Dove (20, 23, 25, 27, 133, 157)
Photos by Peter Dove (7, all cut-outs and Chapters 2, 4, 7, 8 and 10) and Rhett Savoie (Chapters 3, 5,
6, 9 and 11)

Design by Paul Saunders; layout by Kenilworth Press

# Contents

# Foreword | Heather Blitz

YOU HOLD IN YOUR HANDS AN INCREDIBLE KEY to help you unlock the many mysteries of effective, successful and satisfying riding. Before I discovered Mary Wanless and her research into rider biomechanics and learning processes, I fell into a class of riders who have natural talent but not the awareness to use it in the best ways. I was making many relatively common mistakes that could have led me down many long, dead-end roads. These mistakes often go unnoticed in traditional, less thorough teaching – or they are mistakenly accepted. As I continue to follow my goals of riding for the USA in Olympic competition, I find what I have learned from Mary becoming even more important.

Mary's abilities and research are truly unique in the way they help the rider

Heather Blitz in piaffe with Otto.

to lay a foundation of skill, and to develop an in-depth awareness. By learning in this way over time the rider develops a set of 'tools', and having conscious access to these gives me a huge advantage in this infinitely challenging quest for success in international Grand Prix dressage competition. Mary pioneered this realistic and highly do-able system to help all riders from beginners to riders like myself. Her work is equally beneficial to trainers and riding instructors looking for more tools to better help their students. Her understanding of how a rider's biomechanics affects the horse is unprecedented, and unsurpassed. It is also completely necessary for fair and effective training, whatever the level of the rider. Training techniques and exercises can change constantly and might be different with each horse, but biomechanics and the laws of physics stay consistent, from day to day, and from horse to horse. It makes the most remarkable difference to know how this works!

I dream that one day, learning these principles will become universally mandatory – that all riders will have to master them before being allowed a 'licence' to ride. After reading this book, you'll be one huge leap closer to a level of riding you've only dreamed about. Congratulations and good luck!

HEATHER BLITZ

# Acknowledgements

MANY PEOPLE HAVE PLAYED A PART in the creation of this book. Back through time, Ann Mansbridge, my original editor at Methuen, and William and Sandra Papke, who directed and produced my videos (now DVDs) were the people who enabled me to bring my work to the world stage. Without their faith in me and their considerable expertise, it and I would still be virtually unknown. I owe you all so much, and really appreciate our enduring friendships. Thank you.

In the intervening years my publishers at Kenilworth Press in the UK and Trafalgar Square Books in the USA have done a great job on all of my books, and I particularly thank my editor Lesley Gowers and publisher Andrew Johnston for making this new book so wonderfully clear and attractive.

I also want to thank my photographers Peter Dove and Rhett Savoie, who were both patient, creative, and attentive through a long day of lessons. Rhett took photographs in Wellington, Florida, and Peter took photographs here in the UK and in Denmark, including the cover photographs and the studio photographs. He also had some great ideas, and created some of the graphics. Despite an enormous workload he went much further than the extra mile to make them all as good as they could be. Thank you, Pete. Thanks, too, to Emma Dove who was volunteered to take part in the studio photographs, and who did so with great professionalism and good humour!

My illustrator Dianne Breeze has an uncanny way of turning ideas and scribbles into beautiful drawings that really show what I wanted to show – thank you, Dianne; and thanks too to Christine Bousfield whose illustrations reproduced from my early books have stood the test of time.

I am also grateful to the people who let us use their arenas for the photoshoots. My neighbours Ulrik Molgaard and Henriette Andersen were very generous in this regard, as was Kristy Lund of Blue Marlin Farm in Wellington, Florida. Thanks also to Page Hinds-Athan for the use of her arena in Wellington, and for her patience as I rearranged her carefully organised clinic! My thanks go to Ove Mortensen for the use of his arena in Esbjerg, and for his generosity during my recent stay in Denmark. Thanks, too, to Inger Recht who housed and fed me as I put the finishing touches to this book.

A number of people at home hold the fort for me as I gad about and immerse myself in projects that leave a trail of other jobs undone. Thanks particularly to Sam Twyman and Karin Major, who put up with my foibles and do a great job at Overdale Equestrian Centre. Without your computer-brain, Karin, and your ability to hang in there and keep smiling, I would be in big trouble (as you know!).

There would be no book without the riders who agreed to take part, and to put themselves in a phenomenally exposing position so that others might learn from their struggles. So a big thank you to Carol Epstein, Jo Cooper, Millie McCoy, Diane Roddick, Sue Dunk, Karin Major, Page Hinds-Athan and Denise O'Reilly. Also, my thanks to John Zopatti, who took part in the Wellington photoshoot, but whose lesson was not included in the book.

Without the photographs of international Grand Prix dressage rider Heather Blitz, this book would be infinitely poorer. Thank you, Heather, for taking me so seriously (after the first half hour of our first lesson!), and for becoming the person who could embody the principles I have discovered in the world arena. I have so appreciated our ongoing friendship and coaching relationship (and love its new twist of going in both directions). I so hope that you will soon become recognised as one of the most skilled riders in the world, and that you will achieve your goal of riding in the Olympics. And, of course, I hope that you will want your biomechanics coach on hand when that happens!

There are now a number of other riders and coaches who have become co-developers of this work, both in the UK and USA. My thanks to all of you for being living proof that this system works, and that we have coaching and riding skills that are learnable and reproducible. Thanks for your support, your innovations, and the sense of community that you give me. Thanks, too, to my clinic organisers in various parts of the world, who play such an important role in my life and work.

MARY WANLESS

# Introduction

THE TWO GREAT PASSIONS OF MY LIFE ARE RIDING AND TRAVELLING, and I have made some epic journeys to various parts of the world. But before I venture into the unknown, I first look at the guide book. One of a well-known series is my particular favourite – perhaps I should branch out, but experience has shown me that these books capture the essence of a place, and enable me to predict what I shall enjoy doing. So I use the book to help me imagine what it will be like, and to decide where I will base myself. I also imagine where I might go from there, both independently and on organised tours. I look at the book again when I first arrive, and then several more times as I struggle to find my way around. These readings are done when I feel the most lost and over-whelmed, and the guide feels utterly invaluable.

Experiencing the reality of the place helps me to decide if what I *thought* might become my favourite haunts actually will – in this I am comparing the words, and my subsequent flights of fantasy, with the reality of my experience. So, as I decide what my priorities will be, my actions are determined by a melding of my own impressions and the written word. I appreciate that this was handed down by other people as a result of their more in-depth experience, so I do not dismiss it lightly (and I trust it more because these particular books are not driven or biased by the need to sell a particular resort or place). But once I am immersed in an experience, the guide book is put to one side. I want to take the trip, not read about the trip and miss the scenery. Afterwards, I read the guide book again to decide if I think the author did a good job – to see how clearly my impressions matched hers – and maybe to ponder over the choices I made, and the places I did not have the time and energy to see.

My hope for you, as you read this book, is that you too are about to embark on a journey. For this is a guide book or map that shows the way from several different starting points towards the goal of skilled riding. But, of course, there is no causal link between holding a map and making a journey. Many people will look at a map just out of interest, finding it fascinating or amusing in its own right. But, hopefully, they know they are merely looking. If they look at a menu, they certainly know that they have not yet eaten the meal – but I am not so convinced that most people who read a book like this realise that (even if they nod, think, giggle or sigh in the face of some stories and some new ideas) the action only happened inside their heads.

As I teach riders and hold demonstrations in the UK and USA, many people ask me to sign one of my books. Often they are newly bought, so I cannot know what fate will befall them. (Over the years a few people have brought me a book to sign, and confessed that it came from a car boot sale – but at least it finally reached an appreciative owner!) Occasionally someone asks me to sign a book that has obviously been well thumbed. It is highlighted and dog-eared, with notes scrawled in the margins, suggesting that my words really meant something to its reader, and that action happened *outside* her head as well as in it. That is my favourite signing experience, and if the spirit moves you, I encourage you to massacre this one in a similar way.

The book begins with a discussion on learning, which sad to say, few of us are naturally very good at. You would think that our schooling might have helped us here, but rarely does it provide a 'user's manual' for the brain. Instead, we are left to get on with it as best we can. Neither does our schooling encourage us to appreciate the difference between being *told* about an experience and actually *having* an experience – in fact, it probably muddles us into thinking that if we have heard about it, then we know about it. But, as I hope you will really begin to appreciate, these are not one and the same – just as the menu and the meal are not the same.

The next chapter (Chapter 2) shows us what highly skilled riding looks like, and questions whether the words that are traditionally used to describe it are actually viable descriptions. It encourages you to look through a different lens to the one you might normally use, as you notice things you might have missed, and questions things you might have assumed. It also makes it clear that even reading and looking at the photographs does not really prepare you for what that experience (or rather, the journey that takes you towards it) might feel like.

The four defaults define the starting points that virtually everyone will begin from. I call them defaults because they are the setting your body will revert back to unless it is actively told to do something else. Early on in my learning I imagined that riders would easily evolve out of these, but now I think this is rarely the case. Some riders are very stuck in one default, while others ping-pong between the extremes that are possible; but either way, most of us find that those defaults come back to haunt us even when we think we should have banished them. So, in using this book, one of the most important factors is to define your starting point, so that you follow the right map in the right direction. The other descriptions will, I hope, teach you more through the contrasts they provide – and perhaps they will help you to diagnose yourself if you overdo a correction and slip into another of the defaults.

If you enjoy reading this book, and especially if you decide to use it as a guide to help you change your riding, you might also want to read the *Ride With Your*

*Mind Essentials* book (published in 2001). This summarises the main points of the basics, along with the common pitfalls and misunderstandings. *For the Good of the Rider* (published in 1998) puts flesh on the bones, illustrating the theory with short vignettes about a number of riders, and explaining more about fitness, and the challenges that learning presents for both the body and the mind. Going further back through time, *Ride With Your Mind Masterclass* (1991) is a book similar to this one, which illustrated the experience of a number of riders. It is the book where I really found my voice, and it is my personal favourite. My first book *Ride With Your Mind* (published in the USA as *The Natural Rider*, 1987) really showed how shocked I was when I realised that the map I had been given of the territory of riding was really not very helpful – and this shock mirrors the experience of many riders when they first encounter my work.

As I have written these guide books over the years, my knowledge of the territory I describe has obviously increased in depth and scope. But that does not negate the usefulness of those early books. They were written at a time when I did not have the overview I have now, but their value lies in the fact that my struggles back then were almost certainly closer to your own. This 'student's eye view' of the problem has immense value. It mirrors the way that your classmate could empathise with your problem when you could not fathom a maths lesson, making her – and not your teacher – your best source of help when you could not do your homework.

My initial discovery, made in 1980, was really about the importance of core muscle strength, although I did not use that term, which was coined by the fitness world much later. Most people assumed I must be nuts as I started discussing the trouble riders got into by trying to relax. Now, the need for core strength in riding has been taken up by many more people, as has the idea of sitting in 'neutral spine'. Back in 1980, when I felt like a lone wolf crying in the wilderness, these ideas alone were enough to change my riding and my pupils' riding dramatically, and to spur me into writing that first book.

All that I have learned since has been built on those concepts – and as starting points they open the door to much more power, precision and possibility than you might at first imagine. The intervening twenty-eight years of learning has enabled me to coach riders of international standing, like our model Heather Blitz, and this might just put me in a position where the riding world takes me seriously. But it also takes me further from the experience of the average rider, creating the possibility that I too will fall into the biggest pitfall in the horse world, and will presuppose things that are givens for me, but not for her.

All that remains is for me to apologise for my convention of calling the rider 'she' and the horse 'he'. This makes my task in writing far easier, and it also acknowledges that I am writing for an audience that is predominantly female. However, I mean no disrespect to male riders and female horses, who I hope will forgive me and not take offence.

Bon voyage!

# PART 1

# RIDE WITH YOUR MIND

On learning

The model: walk, trot and canter

# CHAPTER 1

# On learning

MOST OF US BEGIN LEARNING TO RIDE inspired by the beauty and grace of horses. We are drawn to their gentleness, and awed by their power. But we are inspired as well by a dream. As a young child, my dream was just to sit on the back of a pony (I thought no further than this) and my vision of riding evolved from that initial delight. It was moulded by the local riding school, and by the trekking holidays that filled my dreams for fifty-one weeks of each year! For all of us, that initial dream is influenced by the culture we are born into, and by our own personal bias – so it may become a longing to gallop off into the sunset, to soar over fences, or to don a top hat and tails. But whichever path you choose, you will find that it is strewn with obstacles that you could never have imagined. When we first begin riding, we are in a state of innocence where we cannot know what there is to know, so it is just not possible to have any idea of the trials and tribulations – as well as the thrills and the spills – that await us.

Some people ride for years, and remain happy to survive with few skills. Riding is then a push–pull affair, involving horses who often seem (by nature) to be stubborn and recalcitrant. Sometimes rider and horse find a happy compromise, but often this evolves as the rider sets her sights *lower*. Perhaps she settles for becoming what we British call a 'happy hacker'. But even this rider/horse relationship, which is designed to minimise the stress on both parties, can still be less than happy. For the riders who want *more*, each of the sporting disciplines provides a progressive set of competitive challenges that are based on stages of training; but the truth is that very few people progress beyond the lower levels. This is not just due to lack of money, desire, or opportunity. It is due to lack of skill – but in many cases this does not equate to lack of time invested, or lack of hard work. Sadly, many 'serious' riders are stuck in a place that falls far short of their dream. Furthermore, the angst involved in getting there has often made their riding far *too* serious.

In English riding, dressage training underlies all of the other disciplines, and there is a theory about how horse and rider should progress up the levels. The practice, however, may be very different. The discrepancy was summed up beautifully by the husband of an aspiring dressage rider, who was a friend of a friend in America. His idea was to write a book about his wife's experience, and its provisional title was 'Ten Years at Training Level'! (this is known by British readers as preliminary level). So do riders get stuck because they themselves are inadequate, or because the theory is inadequate? In its stated form, I believe that the theory is an ideal that can be applied only to the small percentage of riders who are talented. The theory describes what *should* happen, but not what does happen – but it seems that I say this as a lone voice crying in the wilderness, for it is an admission that is not good for the *status quo* of the horse world, and not good for business.

When riders are encouraged to 'buy this schoolmaster, and you will soon be competing at the upper levels', or told that 'this young horse has the talent to take you all the way...', the tacit assumption is that the rider's skill will naturally develop if only she has the right horse. But for people to live their dreams, it takes more than a lovely horse. It takes skills. Since the existing theory of riding works well enough for the talented riders who *could* compete those horses, they see nothing wrong with it – and the riders who cannot put theory into practice usually end up blaming fate or themselves. Sadly, they are often reinforced in their self-abnegation by trainers/instructors/teachers who think nothing of blaming them too. The problem, laid out fair and square, is that they just do not have enough talent.

But this is not fair, or square. As I see it, the biggest lack in the horse world is not lack of opportunity, desire, dedication, or talent. It is lack of 'HOW TO'. How do you get a horse 'on the bit'? How do you 'sit deep' or 'use your back'? How do you ride shoulder-in? The question 'How?' is answered through what sport psychologists call procedural knowledge (which tells you how to proceed) but there is very little of this in the horse world. We do, however, have reams of declarative knowledge, which tells us what horse and rider should look like. When a trainer or instructor says, 'The horse should be on the bit', 'Make him rounder', or 'He needs more bend to the inside', she is using declarative commands which presuppose that the rider knows what to do. But these commands are not 'bite-size chunks' for the many riders who do not know! They are also not 'bite-size chunks' for the many riders who have to be told them again and again, suggesting that their (procedural) strategy for achieving these goals simply does not work.

So are the explanations that we are conventionally given adequate to serve as a 'road map' for the aspiring rider? I think not, yet I am always amazed by how few riders ask for explanations of phrases that sound, to me, like gobbledegook. (It has to be said, however, that 'stupid' questions are rarely encouraged in riding arenas!) Our typical phrases are – to say the least – ambiguous, inviting both contortions and push–pull tactics. 'This hand here and that leg there' is a more accessible explanation than many, but it too is limited in its success, even when people can physically do what they are told. My contention is that all of these phrases do not represent a viable attempt to explain the crucial elements of what good riders actually do.

There is a big schism in the horse world between riders who *do not know what they do*, and riders who *do not do what they know*. One group has working knowledge or 'know-how', and the other group has conceptual knowledge. For many riders, there is nothing more frustrating than to have read the books, watched the videos, been to the seminars, and been told – perhaps countless times – but still to find that they cannot do it. However much theoretical knowledge each of us has gleaned from this exposure, it does not enable us to translate theory into practice, developing the implicit knowledge of the skilled performer, for that requires a different part of the brain. For the last forty years, this schism has usually been attributed to the difference in functioning of the two brain hemispheres.

The typical description tells us that the left brain hemisphere reads the books, hears the words, and knows the theory. Its conceptual or declarative knowledge describes what horse and rider should look like, defining the 'what' of riding, but not the 'how'. Meanwhile, riding skills are the brainchild of the right brain hemisphere, which is the creative, artistic side of the brain. Its only 'languages' are images, rhythms, and 'feelages', and thus the part of the brain that deals in 'know-how' does not understand words. When it comes to practical improvement, this renders all possible book-learning obsolete, and leaves the right brains of many of us unable to do what the left brain knows (we should do).

Meanwhile, the trainers and talented riders – the ones who do not know what they do – have impressive right brain skills that are, to use the official term, 'cognitively impenetrable'. They function out of consciousness, and cannot be taken apart and described by the left brain in language. Hence these riders do not know (in words) what they do (using the implicit know-how of the right brain). This model of the roles of the two brain hemispheres offers a very helpful explanation of phenomena we have all experienced; but over recent years, MRI scans of various people doing various tasks have shown that the reality is much more complex than this. There is a lot of individuality concerning the areas of the brain that are involved in different tasks, and typically, skilled performers perform a task using less of their brain. So to enable me to write about this in a different – and perhaps more useful – way, I am going to draw from the model proposed by Professor Guy Claxton, visiting professor of Education and Psychology at Bristol University.

In his book *Hare Brain, Tortoise Mind* he talks about the 'wordscape' and the 'brainscape', as shown in **Fig. 1.1** (overleaf). In the brainscape, where we are dealing with neurological functioning, it is as if repeated actions carve out hollows or ravines in its surface. It is often said that 'neurons that fire together wire together', and as neural networks are activated, so their repeated use builds the neurological pathways that connect the brain to various muscles. This process is rather like cutting a pathway through long grass, and (in the brain as

**Fig. 1.1**
The brainscape and the wordscape, showing how only a few of the co-ordinations of the brainscape can be described in words, while only a few of the words used in the conventional language of the wordscape are connected to co-ordinations.

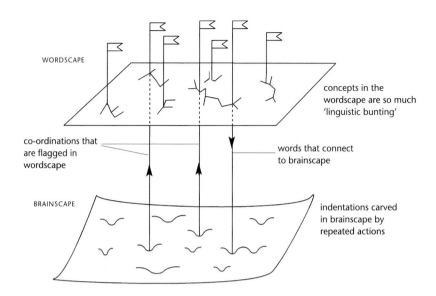

well as the grass) it soon it becomes so much easier to keep using the existing pathway than it is to cut another one. Thus we all develop habit patterns – which may, of course, be the basis of more or less skilful actions.

Some of those co-ordinations in the brainscape send up a long flagpole, as it were, to the wordscape, so they can be 'flagged' and described in language; but many do not, and this means that the implicit knowledge or know-how of the brainscape remains inaccessible to the wordscape. But alongside the practical development of our skills, we are all the recipients of both the formal and the informal education that teaches us, in language, about a particular field of knowledge. This develops the wordscape, and at this level you can think of ideas being linked together by flags that form 'linguistic bunting'. But many of these words do not have an accompanying indentation in the brainscape, just as many of the indentations in the brainscape are not flagged in the wordscape.

While language can liberate us hugely, it brings with it a set of snares that may have become apparent to you as you read the above. Claxton quotes writer Aldous Huxley who stated that 'every individual is at once both the beneficiary and the victim of the linguistic tradition into which he has been born – the beneficiary inasmuch as language gives access to the accumulated records of other people's experience; the victim insofar as it ... bedevils his sense of reality, so that he is all too apt to take his concepts for data, his words for real things'. Claxton adds that 'The topography of each "plane", the brainscape and the wordscape, and the relationship between them, represents an evolving compromise between the erosion of the brainscape by first-hand experience, and the dictates of a particular language about what segments and groupings are to be named.'

These are powerful ideas, with huge implications for the horse world. The dictates of our linguistic tradition determine what 'segments and groupings are to be named', but my contention is that the traditional language of riding bears very little connection to the implicit knowledge in the brainscape of a skilled rider. Furthermore, when people talk about riding just from the 'linguistic bunting' of the wordscape they cannot begin to do it justice, and the chances are that they are simply 'reciting the catechism'.

Twenty-eight years ago, when I began to delve into this schism between language and experience, I felt like the child in the story of The Emperor's New Clothes; now I state with some authority that (as Guy Claxton puts it so beautifully) 'the dislocation between expertise and explanation' that exists within the horse world comes at a huge price. It leaves many riders feeling stupid and incapable, and it limits the skills of the masses (whether they realise it or not) in a way that makes me lament on their behalf. It also limits the skills of even the best riders in the world, who have stumbled upon some aspects of the possible skills of the brainscape, but who could extend their skills even further if only their trainers used words in more helpful ways.

To bring these ideas to life, think of a time when you discovered a good new 'feelage' in your riding, and then found that a phrase that was used by an instructor perhaps days, months or even *years* before popped into your head. As you found yourself thinking, 'So that's what she meant!', what really happened was that words which were just so much linguistic bunting suddenly became connected to that 'feelage' in the brainscape. What an exciting moment, and how remarkable it is that the experience is powerful enough to bring that phrase to mind! Or you may be one of the riders who has been told 'Heels down' for years, but who has experienced very little improvement. Then one day you find yourself in front of a trainer who says 'Toes up', and on goes the light bulb! The phrase has meaning, through the way it connects the wordscape with the brainscape. To quote a phrase from my childhood, it makes 'the penny drop'. Strange as it may seem, a tiny change in the language used can catalyse that connection, but as you are probably aware, years of repeatedly being told the same thing are highly unlikely to yield anything other than a seed that falls – yet again – on the stony ground of the wordscape.

Few riders with a highly skilled brainscape have made any effort to link the two planes, which means that they cannot discuss their skills or pass them on. This is a huge loss for us as their pupils; but it is also a loss for them as riders. Research has shown that the implicit know-how of the brainscape is relatively inflexible, and that it may fail to transfer to a different situation even when the underlying logic remains the same. If you can take your skill apart, reflect on it, and put it back together in a slightly novel way, you have much more chance of coming up with the skills that are needed to match a changing situation. Also, if you can discuss your skill with others, your collective brain-power may find new solutions to old problems. But even without that outside help, experiments have also shown that conscious reflection (which relies on a link between the brainscape and the wordscape) increases your ability to see that some aspect of what you have learned in one situation is relevant to another, even though the situations may superficially look different.

As a rider and coach my role has firstly been to build good riding skills in the brainscape, and alongside this to make, maintain, and develop links between the brainscape and the wordscape. This helps me to find ways of making those links for others – whatever level they ride at. This approach has required me to question our traditional language, and as I have observed my pupils and discussed my thoughts with them, we have collectively built a terminology that names and describes some different segments of experience to our traditional language. I believe that it forms a linkage between the two planes that can evolve as the rider's skill evolves, that has its own logic, and that makes the skills of riding much more accessible and transferable. Furthermore, I believe that riders limit themselves hugely when *they think only what is thinkable within the conventional language of the wordscape.*

In my previous books, I wrote about learning by using the 'conscious competence' model. When riders enter my riding arena for the first time they are usually in the state of being 'unconscious of their incompetence', which means that they *do not know what they do not know*. We often say that 'ignorance is bliss' – and sometimes this is true – but it is certainly true that for most people, becoming conscious of their incompetence is a difficult experience. ('You're telling me that I can't even do rising trot properly, after all of these years? And that I have to do that "bearing down" thing… this is horrible!') Next follows the stage of becoming consciously competent, where the rider needs to keep giving herself reminders that help her to choose the new pattern over the old. This is often said to take *ten thousand repetitions* of an action, and it is the time where the brainscape has its strongest connection to the wordscape – in effect, the rider knows (and can describe in language) what she knows (in her brainscape). But elite riders, who have a highly developed nervous system, do it much faster than this, quickly relegating that skill to the implicit knowledge of the brainscape. Once a skill is ingrained enough to function on 'automatic pilot', the rider reaches the stage of unconscious competence, where she no longer knows (in language) what she knows (in her brainscape).

The early stages of my learning are thoroughly imprinted on all levels of my brain as I learned – excruciatingly slowly – how to bear down, and to find my left seat bone, stay on axis, etc. Eventually, as insights and discoveries began to come thick and fast, so 'feelages' began to evolve increasingly quickly, metamorphosing and building on each other in a way that makes individual stages much harder to flag. The kind of change that would once have taken me months to ingrain and understand may now be ingrained in one ride. I see this too in elite riders, and on one level I am extremely pleased to have joined their ranks!

But the downside is that stages in learning are much more easily forgotten, and as 'unconscious competence' takes over, the flagpoles that connected the brainscape with the wordscape will wither and die. I do all that I can to keep my learnings accessible to the wordscape, because my main aim is to build a model not just of elite riding skills, but of the way in which riding skills develop. However, it is much more common for coaches to surrender to unconscious

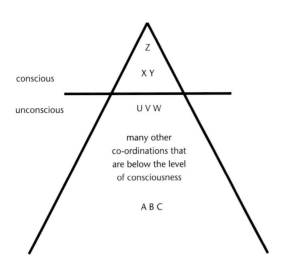

competence, allowing themselves to forget. Most of us look back at our lives and think, 'If only I'd known then what I know now'; however, I sometimes find myself looking at coaches and thinking, 'If only they knew now what they knew then....', for the skills they have forgotten are the skills their pupils need to learn. In their teaching, they then start to *presuppose* those skills instead of teaching them explicitly. In effect, they are teaching the pupil as if they were teaching themselves.

Let us imagine a naturally gifted rider who really wants to pass on her skills, but who has had few struggles in the phase of 'conscious competence'. Many of her skills came naturally, and she never deliberately 'flagged' those that she did have to learn. So the skills of her brainscape lie submerged in her unconscious mind. It is as if they imagine them buried within the seven-eighths of the iceberg that lie submerged below the surface of the sea. **(Fig. 1.2)** Only the most recently acquired elements of that rider's skill (much less than one-eighth) are flagged in her wordscape, and they remain available to the surface levels of consciousness for as long as she remains 'conscious of her competence'. In her riding, if she can hold those together, she holds the whole iceberg together, and she never needs to worry about the rest of it. (What an enviable situation!) So the biggest problem is that if she tells us about its tip – which is all she can tell us about if she is to talk from personal experience – those insights will only help us if we too have the equivalent iceberg. If we do not, we will not be able to utilise them, for we are being given the XYZs before we have built a foundation of ABCs.

It is my belief that many of the phrases that are assumed to be the ABCs of riding are actually XYZs. This is quite logical, given that they must once have come out of the mouths of the world's most revered riders, as 'tip of the iceberg' phrases that linked their brainscape to their wordscape. For many who hear them, they remain as linguistic bunting. More assiduous souls, however, actively seek ways to link these words to feelings in the brainscape. But they do so without the implicit knowledge of that gifted rider, and as I see it, the 'feelages' that seem to be the obvious interpretation of phrases like 'grow up tall and stretch your legs down', 'stick your chest out', 'push your heels down', or 'use your back' are a far cry from the original feelages those elite riders wanted to convey. The discrepancies are so huge that they thwart the attempts of many riders who are longing to become more skilled.

The word 'talent' alludes to that hidden part of the iceberg – to the skills of the brainscape that came naturally without work or thought. 'Talent' really means 'She's very good at it but we don't know why', and there will always be some indefinable element that makes Kyra Kyrklund perform like Kyra Kyrklund, and makes John Whitaker perform like John Whitaker. There are some indefinable elements that make Heather Blitz (our model in this book) ride like Heather Blitz. But if we look in the right way, we can define much more than we commonly suppose. In most of the equestrian disciplines, the scoring system ignores the rider and looks only (or mainly) at the horse, and sadly, this biases the entire training system to consider the horse as the athlete, and the rider as incidental. But riders are not incidental. As it became clear to me that they, and their skills, are pivotal to their horses' performance, so I made it my job to look not as the judges look, but with an 'eye' that reads the rider's body and her interaction with her horse.

Twenty-eight years of looking, listening and feeling might be considered very 'low tech', but it has led to a model that links theory and practice, conceptual and working knowledge, the wordscape and the brainscape, in some beautiful ways. Without the traditional 'dislocation between expertise and experience' we have a route map that can take many more riders beyond the basics and closer to their dream. It is a much more rider-friendly and forgiving system, even though it is extremely precise. For it needs to be as precise as the laws of physics, and as precise as the ways in which a horse reads and reacts to his rider's body. It is a paradigm shift that can revolutionise the field, one rider at a time, beginning with those who – like the riders in this book – are willing to think 'out of the box' in order to live their dreams.

Within this model, we need explanations that will work for riders at different levels, be they children, teenagers, riders who know they are struggling, or riders who think they know more than they do. We could be coaching a club level competitor still attempting to move beyond those ubiquitous basics, or a skilled rider working at a high level of sophistication. As an overview (and this is true of any field of knowledge) the more simple we make any explanation, the less *accurate* it becomes, and the more *accurate* we make our explanation, the less *simple* it becomes. Anyone who has struggled to read and understand scientific papers has experienced first-hand the truth of this! The relationship between accuracy and simplicity is shown in the graph below. (**Fig. 1.3**) As is also shown on this graph, what we really need is a series of explanations that we can offer to riders at different levels, gradually homing in on 'the truth' as we add accuracy, and forsake the simplicity that children and novices need to get them started. For anything more would be overwhelming.

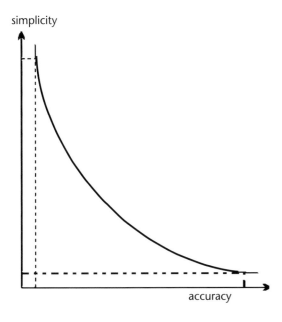

simplicity

accuracy

Fig. 1.3
The relationship between simplicity and accuracy in a theory or map of riding.

key
-------- The very simple explanation is not very accurate.
– – – – The very accurate explanation is not very simple.

(After Peter Coltrane, *Uncommon Sense*, Capstone 2004)

Within the horse world, no one considers that there might be a progression that describes how the rider learns to sit – that sitting can be described with varying degrees of accuracy, as a skill that is built in layers. There is an established progression that takes the horse up the levels, and teaches him more athletic movements etc.; but there is no similar progression for the development of the rider. But even within trot on a twenty-metre circle, that progression exists, and it yields the skills (of half-halts, bend, or collection) that are presupposed in the rider when a trainer or judge outlines the ideal progression for the horse. This is the great omission in the horse world. Even in the classical schools, with their hours spent riding on the lunge, the learning of these skills was still largely down to chance or innate talent. But they can be learned explicitly, and in 'bite-size chunks' that build on each other as the rider homes in on the accuracy and precision of a highly integrated nervous system.

I like to compare learning to ride well with peeling the layers of an onion. None of us can go straight to its centre; instead we have to learn the lessons of each layer in turn. As you reach each next layer, your simpler explanation becomes a more accurate and detailed one – but because you are ready to hear it, and because it solves the problem more effectively, it does not seem like an imposition. Instead, the seed drops down to the fertile ground of the brainscape, and yields a revelation. Ideally the rider experiences revelation, upon revelation, upon revelation as each layer of the onion reveals its secrets. I do not mean to imply that learning will be a smooth and easy progression, and there may well be fallow patches and frustrations, times when you lose your way, and times when your progress seems blocked. But there will also be times when a quantum leap takes you to a new layer, and you suddenly discover a new horizon. This is life-long learning at its best; but while learning to ride well is one of the most challenging and satisfying journeys there is, it is not – even with the refinement that I can bring to it – a journey for the faint-hearted.

Fig. 1.4
The learning process can be
compared to peeling the
layers of an onion. Some
flaws extend deep into the
layers, and fatal flaws extend
all the way to its centre.

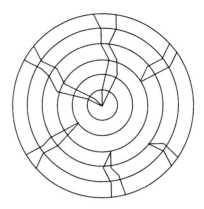

**Figure 1.4** shows this onion diagrammatically, and it also shows (metaphorically) how we have flaws and fatal flaws. None of us has the perfect body for riding, and we all have our cross to bear – whether it be a funny right wrist, a wobbly left leg, or some other variation on the theme. That 'cross' may be more or less challenging depending on how talented we are, but either way, few of these issues are resolved in the outer layers of learning. Many of the issues follow us through the layers, becoming more subtle as each layer of learning yields a fix that can seem fantastic at the time. But it will soon be revealed (by your dear friend the horse) as only a partial solution to the problem. Gradually we come closer to the core of issue, but we may not fully eradicate it – for even in the able-bodied and talented, some of these issues come right from the centre of the onion.

However, as I see it, the onion actually has no centre, for there is no such thing as 'arriving'. There is always something more to learn, for there is no end to the changes in perception that can yield slightly different – and more effective – ways to organise muscles. Thus you can think and feel your way into refinements that keep fine-tuning your performance, even if you are already one of the world's best riders. The endless possibilities of refinement are represented by the endless layers that grow from the centre of the onion. Those fatal flaws, though smaller now, may well grow with them – until, one day, perhaps, even they grow out.

As you learn the lessons of each layer, so you have to do the dedicated practice that ingrains each new co-ordination in the brainscape. Each new phase begins with the 'Aha!' moment that first connects the wordscape to the brainscape, and then each new co-ordination requires those ten thousand repetitions through which you get it, and lose it, and get it, and lose it, until you get it more and lose it less. You get it faster, get it easier, and get it clearer – and eventually you get it so that you can stop yourself from losing it, and you get it so that you never have to think about it again.

Meanwhile, you are playing a game with your horse that I call the 'got it/lost it' game, in which he is the teacher who tells you that you have got it, and lost it, and got it, and lost it. You feel your own body change, and you feel his body change in response. I call this 'riding on interface', because you are not thinking just about yourself (and practising your position) and not thinking just about him (and training your horse). This perceived schism between two alternatives is all but endemic in the horse world, but it is highly misleading and destructive. In the 'got it/lost it' game you work on *yourself and your horse simultaneously*. Both of you are training neurological patterns, training responsiveness, training awareness, and training muscles. Through this interaction with him you get to reinvent the wheel, discovering what others have discovered before you. It may seem laborious and inefficient, but it is the only way. *Being told about the wheel* will only embellish your wordscape.

While riders have the fantasy of 'arriving', 'riding on interface' is actually all there is. You may ride for thirty years, and throughout that time you keep getting it and losing it, and getting it and losing it. The only differences as time progresses are the subtlety of the 'it' that you get and lose, and the precision of the nervous system through which you process that information. This process yields the endless layers of learning that are not the way most people think about riding or training horses. Many riders think that they, as the superior human, do not need feedback from a supposedly inferior horse. On the contrary; it is the horse who needs to learn their language (and obey their aids) not they who need to listen to him and learn his.

The graph in **Fig. 1.5** shows skills plotted against time for the average and the talented rider who are both learning through conventional means. Both performers reach a stage where they keep doing the same things (often harder) as they keep being told the same words (often louder); but this leaves them stuck on a plateau. Since neither rider has unlocked the skill of 'learning how to learn' their performances level off, albeit at different levels.

**Figure 1.6** shows the same variables plotted for riders who are explicitly learning the biomechanical skills that can take them through the layers. Concurrently they 'learn how to learn', so they learn how to teach themselves, and also to appreciate the horse as their teacher. Over the years I have become a fantastic learner, but I confess to being a rider who is 'average + skilled'. I love to ride, I keep discovering more sophisticated skills, and I keep thinking 'out of the

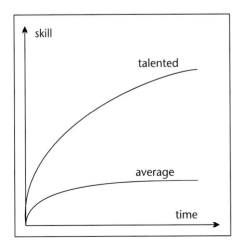

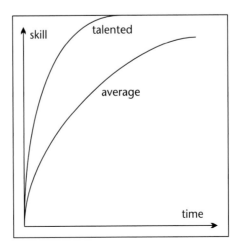

Fig. 1.5 *(far left)*
The learning curves of the average and talented rider, using traditional instruction based on declarative statements.

Fig. 1.6 *(left)*
The learning curves of the average and talented rider who develop their procedural knowledge and learn specific skills.

(After Robert Dilts, *Modelling with NLP*, Metapublications, 1998) box', as I find better ways to describe those skills in language. But if I go to the Olympics it will be on my feet as a biomechanics coach and sport psychologist. Heather Blitz, whom you will meet in the next chapter, is 'talented + skilled'; the implicit skills of her brainscape spared her some of the learnings that took me years. She can perform the skills I have shown her in a more robust body–mind than my own, and with an equal or more sophisticated perception. She has conscious access to skills that other top-class riders cannot even dream about.

But all of us, whatever level we ride at, benefit from having a better link between conceptual and working knowledge. This means we can travel with the help of a much more accurate map, and this makes our journey much less stressful. Not only are we are less likely to get lost, we can have much more fun as well!

# CHAPTER 2

# The model: walk, trot and canter | Heather

I FIRST MET HEATHER IN 1994, through the ingenuity of one of her pupils, who began our story by going, one rainy day, to a horse show. As the heavens opened she took shelter in the book stall, and began browsing through my first book, *Ride With Your Mind*. Her interest was piqued enough for her to buy it, and she subsequently thought, 'I want to be taught like this!' So she contacted the group of friends who were Heather's pupils, and arranged for them to club together and pay for Heather to fly to California, where she attended one of my teacher training courses.

I met Heather properly a year later, when I was invited to teach in Louisiana by another professional. Then I remembered the tall, attractive woman who had sat quietly at the back (in a way not typical of Americans), giving me very little indication about what she was thinking. Heather and some of her pupils rode on that clinic, and in Heather's first lesson it was immediately obvious that while she had done a very good job on her students, she had missed some important points on herself. It was also immediately obvious that she had what it takes to ride unusually well.

Our first lesson was so pivotal that I wrote about it in *For the Good of the Rider*. Heather began it leaning back and 'growing tall', showing the same default as Diane in Chapter 6. I took her stirrups up three holes, and began working very hard – against considerable resistance – to convince her to drop her ribs down towards her hips. She confessed later that when she eventually did as I was asking, she was actually thinking, 'I'll just humour her. She'll give up on this soon!' But as I persisted, her horse showed her the value of the changes she was making, and she gradually became much easier to teach. That was the beginning of a great friendship and teaching relationship, which has now lasted twelve years, with Heather attending between one and three clinics per year.

Arabella, the horse featured in the final chapter, was born in 1997 at Oak Hill Stud, Louisiana, and is by the Danish stallion Rambo. In 1998 Heather began to work for Richard Freeman who owns the stud, backing and training the young horses bred there. But her job description changed radically when Richard brought Rambo to America. Under Richard's ownership he had lived in Denmark, where he was reserve on the Danish Dressage team in the Barcelona Olympics. When he arrived in Louisiana in 1999 he was aged twelve, and he provided Heather with her first competitive rides at Grand Prix. She had previously trained her own horse to Intermediare 1; but taking on a horse trained by someone else proved extremely challenging. It was a make-or-break situation in which she found herself having nightmares and wishing that he would just disappear – but despite this she soon found herself ranked at tenth place in the USA.

Arabella, who was nine when these photographs were taken, is owned by Denise Arroyo. Here too lies an unusual story. Denise was a pupil of Heather's who went, just for fun, to the breed inspection day where a panel of judges from Denmark were grading the horses bred at the stud. There she saw Arabella as a foal, and thought 'Look at that lovely little chestnut ballerina! I have to have her!' Denise works as a teacher at a children's hospital, and lacking a large stash of cash, she asked Richard if she could make a down-payment and put Arabella on 'layaway'. He said 'Yes' … and three years later it became Heather's job to start Arabella, who soon proved far too much horse for Denise to ride herself. So out of the most un-horsey part of America, with the most unlikely owner and coach, comes a horse bred for the job but ridden by an unknown rider. In 2006 this partnership emerged, apparently from nowhere, as a contender for the American dressage team.

Also a contender for the team is Otto, the horse featured in this chapter. He is an eleven-year-old gelding, also by the Danish stallion Rambo and out of a mare by Rampal. He was also bred in Louisiana. As an eight-year-old he came to Heather for training, in the hope that this would make him easier for his owner – to this point he had done very little, but had proved a spirited, difficult ride. Just as Heather was starting to fall for him his owner decided to sell, and Heather began looking for someone who would buy him for her to train and compete seriously. This took some time, and it was Ove Mortensen, one of her Danish contacts, who came up trumps. Since the summer of 2006 Heather and both horses have been living in Denmark and competing on the European circuit. The photos of Otto were taken there in the summer of 2007, over a year after all the other photos were taken.

It will make far more sense to talk about the content of Heather's lessons in our final chapter. There she rides Arabella in the more advanced work, and demonstrates how the basic principles of correct biomechanics (the ABCs of riding) can be built on to make it possible to ride those movements. Here, we are using her as a model to show those ABCs in walk, rising trot, sitting trot and canter. The value in having a visual model of the goal is that it shows us what we are looking for. However, its limitation is that it cannot tell us what we are feeling for, or how to get from here to there. I can virtually guarantee that if you were able to use this book and your ridden work to turn yourself into a clone of Heather, the journey would involve feeling weird beyond your wildest dreams!

## Walk

**Photo 2.1** shows Heather in walk. It was taken right at the beginning of the session, and Otto has his ears pricked, looking at the view. Heather is biding her time, doing nothing actively to stop this, but just maintaining the textbook straight line from her elbow through the hand and rein to the horse's mouth. Notice how we just see the back of her hands, with her thumb uppermost. Talented riders do not have to deal with the problems of 'funny' wrists and ankles that beset most riders, and I do not think I have ever spoken to Heather about any of these joints. But for many riders they appear to have a life of their own, as they rotate in the strange directions that turn toes and fingers in or out, up or down. Largely through my own riding, and through working with the riders I have coached for a long time, I have come to the conclusion that their actions are the result of aberrations in the rider's ribcage. (Read on, and this connection will begin to seem less bizarre!) The corrections needed to make wrists and ankles look like Heather's are certainly not easy for most riders to make, or, more significantly, to maintain. Will power and obedience cannot do that job.

A basic premise of my understanding of the learning process is that when-

**Photo 2.1**
Heather is riding Otto in walk, right at the start of the session. He is looking at the view, but her hand just maintains the textbook straight line from her elbow to his mouth. Her heel is level with her toe instead of being down.

**Photo 2.2**
Otto is now beginning to reach into the rein. Heather's left heel aims more towards her horse's hock, but the stirrup is under her toe, not under the ball of her foot as it is on the other side.

ever I, or any other teacher, find ourselves reminding the rider again and again and again about the same problem, we are harping on about a symptom and not a cause. There is an underlying 'something' that is holding the issue in place, making it not yet ripe for change. In the case of wrists and ankles, that 'something' is very deep rooted. That does not mean that we should not attempt to improve 'funny' ankles or wrists, and I can add to the mainstream commands a number of tactics that will make them significantly better. But realise that you will drip water on that particular rock for a long time before they naturally hold themselves in the right place, becoming an easy-to-control part of you.

Heather's heel is actually level with her toe instead of being down. In **Photo 2.2**, which shows her left side, it aims more towards the horse's hock. However, the stirrup is under her toe instead of being under the ball of her foot, as it is on the other side. Here we are getting a tiny insight into Heather's asymmetry – which is infinitely less than it is for most riders – and which has been an ongoing focus of our work. Virtually no one looks as symmetrical as she does, and if they do, you can bet that they have worked on it, mitigating the tendency for one knee to point more up, as the foot on that side goes more forward. Neither of Heather's sides is spot-on, for ideally the stirrup would be on the ball of the foot while the heel aims towards the horse's hock; but she has still more than satisfied our most important criteria for good sitting.

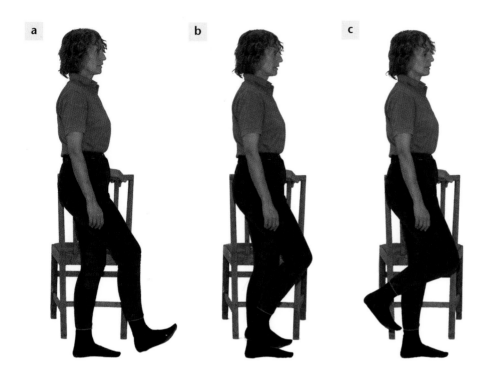

**Fig. 2.1**
If the rider rotates her lower leg from her knee so that it moves like pendulum, her heel will look down if the calf is forward (a). It will look level with the toe when the calf is positioned to give her a shoulder/hip/heel straight vertical line (b), and above the toe when the calf is moved further back (c). However, there has been no change in the ankle joint itself. Any rider who is determined to 'put her heels down' will ride with her lower leg too far forward.

'Heels down' is one of the phrases most commonly heard in riding arenas; and that you should 'keep your heels down' is something everybody knows about riding. But these words encourage people to press hard into the stirrups. By Newton's third law of motion, every action has an equal and opposite reaction; in other words, if you push down, you will experience an equal and opposite push up. This will straighten both your knee and your hip, locking those joints and sending your backside up out of the saddle. Heather's foot *rests* on the stirrup but does not press on it, leaving her joints free to be good shock-absorbers. This enables her to find the right balance between 'up' and 'down'. This is a defining element of her 'bumprint' – which gives her a certain look, and a certain influence. To my eye Heather 'looks right' (which makes me wonder if she also does to yours), but when I first met her she was too 'up'. To understand this clearly you will need to read on, and see the contrasts between her body and those of the riders who began their lesson too 'up' (Carol, Jo, and Diane) or too 'down' (Millie).

Another problem with 'heels down' is that most riders obey the command by pushing their lower leg forward. (See **Fig. 2.1**) Anyone can make their heel look down by aiming it towards the horse's knee, and in jumping this helps to sta-bilise the lower leg (although it is often overdone). But not enough distinction is made in mainstream teaching between the jumping and the flatwork balance. Our main aim here is to keep the rider's centre of gravity over her base of support, and this determines both the alignment of her torso and the position of her feet.

As you look at the photos, ask yourself, 'How would Heather land on the riding arena if the horse were taken out from under her by magic?' On both reins, the answer is that she would land standing on her feet – living proof that her centre of gravity is indeed over her base of support. (You might want to contrast this with the riders' starting points in Chapters 3 to 6.) Most riders have heard of the idea of a shoulder-to-hip-to-heel vertical line, but unlike the idea of 'heels down' few pay more than lip service to it. Here you see it in action. The shoulder seam of Heather's T-shirt is directly above the bony knobble at the top outside of her thigh. This is not the point of the hip; it is the greater trochanter of the femur. To find it on yourself, stand in an 'on-horse' position, and put your fingertips on your panty-line at the top outside of your thigh. If the knobbles are still not clear, lean your torso slowly from side to side. The knobble should protrude under your fingers on the side you are leaning towards. (See **Fig. 2.2**) This bony knobble is in turn directly above the bony knobble in her ankle, which lies just above and behind the eyehole in her spur.

Notice that you can see the intrinsic curves of her spinal column; Heather's neck curves a little forward (and if you wanted to be really 'picky' you could criticise her for having her ear slightly ahead of the shoulder/hip/heel line), while her spine between her shoulder blades curves back, and her waist curves slightly forward. We are all built more or less curvy, but for each skeleton, those curves come into balance when we sit in 'neutral spine'. A factor in Heather's talent is that this comes easily to her; but it was not how she sat when I met her. Sadly fewer than five per cent of riders sit this way, and in the teaching or training they receive few are encouraged to make this their first priority. It is harder to do if your particular skeleton is either unusually curvy, or close to ram-rod straight, but I can hardly begin to describe to you its advantages. **Figure 2.3**

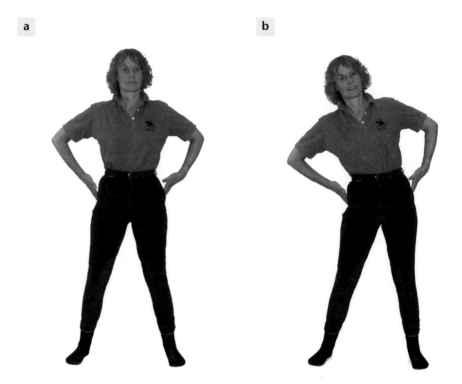

Fig. 2.2
Find the greater trochanter of the femur by standing in an 'on horse' position (a) and putting your fingertips on your panty line at the top outside of your thigh. If the knobbles are still not clear, lean from side to side (b), and you will feel the knobble on the side you are leaning towards.

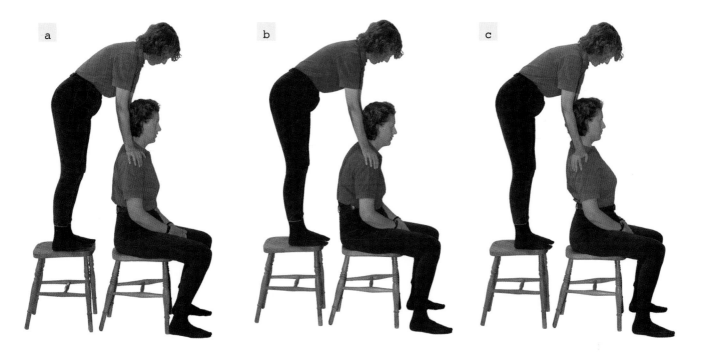

shows the test for neutral spine, but if you attempt this with someone, proceed with caution especially if she is hollow backed. Riding in neutral spine will make you far more likely to remain pain-free through a lifetime of riding, while making you much more efficient, effective, and easier for the horse to carry. But these words do not begin to convey the power of the experience that I hope these pages will reveal.

Is Heather 'growing tall and opening her chest'? Both I and she would say a resounding 'no' – and find ourselves chuckling over our struggle in that first lesson! Before you disagree, realise that if there were an elastic cord from the nape of her neck to her coccyx, and from the centre of her collar bone to her pubic bone, they would both be the same length. Also, (at the risk of being crude) notice that her chest aims to the base of the horse's ears. Most riders who grow tall are making their front cord longer, and aiming their bosom well above the horse's ears. They have become hollow-backed, losing neutral spine and the posture which also defines a skilled martial artist.

Is her 'lower leg on the girth'? While this command is taken very seriously by riders, it is actually extremely vague. Furthermore, the concept conflicts with the idea of a hip-to-heel vertical line, which is also part of our traditional ethos. Few riders seem to have noticed the discrepancy, but I think we have no choice but to reject one of these tenets. I am convinced that the laws of physics determine that the vertical shoulder/hip/heel line is the correct choice, and I hope I can prove that to you as this book (and your own riding) progress.

Has Heather 'relaxed her thigh and taken her knee off the saddle'? To my eye, the answer is a resounding 'no'. This is clarified by **Photo 2.3** (overleaf), which shows her cantering towards the camera. The whole length of her inner thigh is on the saddle, as is the top part of her boot. The rest of her lower leg lies close

**Fig. 2.3**
The test for neutral spine, which should be done by a professional bodyworker who has the skills to manipulate the body into the neutral spine position. Both the tester and the rider must be supported by a safe level surface. In (a) the tester's pressure, which goes vertically down onto the rider's shoulders, does not deform her spine. Instead, they can both feel that it is transmitted through her body all the way down to her seat bones. In (b) she was initially round backed, and the pressure has made her collapse her front more. In (c) she was initially hollow backed and the pressure has made her hollow more. In the latter case it is dangerous to apply anything but a very light pressure, but in neutral spine the body can withstand significant pressure without pain or deformation of the spine.

**Photo 2.3**
As Heather canters towards the camera, we can see how her inner thigh, her knee, and the top of her boot are against the saddle, but her lower leg is slightly away from the horse. Notice that the background is visible between her right calf and the horse.

to the horse rather than against it. In effect, she *moulds* onto the horse with her inner thigh – and, in fact, with skills that lie deep into the layers of the onion, she *moulds the horse onto her with her inner thigh*. This cannot be done without contact. Neither can the thigh support her body weight. This is another of the basics of correct biomechanics, the practice of which puts me, Heather, the Spanish Riding School riders, and virtually all top dressage competitors at odds with the frequently heard dictum that you should 'relax your thighs and take your knees off the saddle'.

At 6 feet tall, Heather makes Otto, at 17hh look an average size, and she makes Arabella, who is 16.2hh look small. In fact, it annoys me intensely that I look smaller on a 14.2hh pony than she does on a 16.2hh horse, and if you too are short, you can stack the odds in your favour by buying a smaller horse who fits you. A bigger horse can still potentially be ridden well, although he will become difficult for a small rider if he is the type who throws his weight around. But realise that if you are 5 foot, you must utilise the same biomechanics as a 6 foot rider, but in miniature. Do not decide that because you are short, you must lengthen your stirrups and make your leg longer. In an ideal world Heather would only ride horses of at least 17hh; but the length of her stirrups has been guided not by her height, but by the need to get her thigh bone at the 45° angle that lies half-way between horizontal and vertical. The bone lies under the midline of her thigh, which is clearly seen in **Photos 2.1** and **2.2**.

This angle makes the rider biomechanically most efficient, enabling the thigh to act as a lever. This is one of the most important unseen and unacknowledged aspects of skilled riding, and you will see the riders in the next four chapters struggling to change how they use their thigh to carry their weight. Sitting well is like standing with your knees bent in a martial arts posture, or like sitting on one of those ergonomic stools that are good for your posture. Here, your thighs and backside rest on a downward slope, while your shins also rest on a slope. It is easy to understand that if the rider's weight is taken predominantly on her backside she squashes the horse's back down, encouraging and perpetuating the hollow that I call the 'man-trap'. It is trickier to appreciate how, just by spreading her weight down through her thigh, she can begin to draw the horse's back up.

To give you a practical understanding of how the thigh muscles produce leverage, stand in an 'on horse' position. If you do this for any length of time you will find that the quadriceps muscles on the front of your thighs begin to ache. If you had a saddle between your legs, some of the strain they experience could be taken by the adductor muscles on the insides of the thighs. Using your thigh muscles to hold you up while riding is very different from surrendering your body weight to the horse and expecting him to hold you up – no muscle work is involved in this, and if you treat the horse like an armchair you squash his back down.

The exact way in which leverage draws the horse's back up will become clear later; suffice it to say right now that having this as an aim means that it is also your aim to cause the horse reach and arch his neck into the rein of his own accord. In other words, when you take care of his back, he takes care of his head and neck, because physiologically, lifting the back and reaching the neck into the rein go together. I call these responses the 'seeking reflexes', and through them the horse seeks contact with the rider's backside and seeks contact with the rein. At the same time he breathes more deeply, and his ribcage fills out to seek contact with his rider's inner thigh. Pulling or fiddling with the reins cannot make these reflexes happen; in fact, any attempt to bring the horse's head down while his back is hollow puts him into a contortion which he will very likely resist.

In both people and horses, hollow backs go with lifted chins, as you can prove to yourself by exaggerating either aspect of this posture, and noticing what happens to the other. Yet most riders are taught to get the horse's head down without concerning themselves with the shape of his back. Thus they become hand-dominant riders, who are doomed to have battles with their horses. The horses who resist the most are the ones with the most integrity, for they will not submit to the contortion. The rest might bring their head down, but they usually look as if they have a huge head rammed into the end of a short, scrawny neck, with a very tight angle under the gullet. Unlike the horse who truly lifts his back and reaches into the rein, this is not a pretty sight. These riders can find that it takes years to unlearn their hand-dominant strategies, and discover how to ride the horse 'from back to front' instead of 'from front to back'.

If you are to develop hands like Heather's – and I have to say that I do not think I have ever seen her draw her hands backwards and pull back on the reins – the muscles of your thigh and torso have to work extremely hard. Yet I doubt if you are looking at her and thinking anything other than, 'She looks nice and relaxed.' Your eyes are deceiving you, and if you were to ask a number of skilled riders what they did with their thighs, their answers would deceive you too. The vast majority would say 'Nothing', which is the most misleading response they could give. To understand this, imagine going into a room that has a smell in it. Regardless of whether the smell is nice or nasty, you smell it strongly at first and then habituate to it. You would then have to go out of the room, breathe some fresh air, and come back into it again in order to rediscover the smell. When a rider tells you that she is doing 'nothing' she is effectively telling you that she 'doesn't smell it any more', and her communication should be taken no more seriously than this. (In other words, do not rush away and try to do nothing!)

For Heather, this position is a very easy neutral, although her thigh muscles might become stressed by a very difficult horse, and/or the more advanced work. However, because she has a conscious understanding of the mechanics of her body and muscle use, she could tell you about the way in which she uses her thigh muscles to support her body weight. She would also appreciate that her 'nothing' might be a very big 'something' for you – as it was for most of the riders in this book

## Rising trot

**Photos 2.4–2.6** show three phases of rising trot. The nicest photograph is **Photo 2.6**, which is taken close to the moment of half-way-up or half-way-down. This puts the horse's legs into the most photogenic position, and in the exact moment when one pair of legs is maximally reaching forward and the other pair is maximally extended back, we are able to see if the horse is tracking up. This happens when the advancing hind hoof steps exactly into the hoof print left by the forefoot which is about to advance, and this is one of the definitions of working trot. Here, Otto has not quite reached this stage in the stride, but as he is in collected trot (with shorter, more elevated steps) we would not expect him to track up.

The rider is maximally 'up' or 'down' when one pair of legs is vertical, and this is the definition of mid-stance. **Photo 2.4** hits this moment more precisely than **Photo 2.5**. You would not choose either picture to frame and hang on your wall (and photographers train themselves to capture a moment close to **Photo 2.6**). However, the photographs are instructive for what they show us about a

Photos 2.4–2.6
Here we see the three phases of rising trot. The nicest photograph is Photo 2.6, which is taken close to the moment of half-way-up or half-way-down.

biomechanically correct rising trot mechanism. In this, the rider's knee acts like the centre point of a circle. The thigh bone is then a radius of that circle, and the greater trochanter of the femur moves forward and up along an arc of the circle. Nothing from the knee down changes, and you can see in the photographs that Heather's lower leg has not moved. What may be less obvious is that there is also barely any more weight in her stirrups as she rises.

It is interesting, too, to look at the angle of her upper body. At the top of the rise she comes very close to having a straight vertical line up the front of her body, from her knee to her hip to her shoulder. If we took her horse out from under her by magic, she would land on her feet on the riding arena, which demonstrates that she is still in balance. As will become clear in the later chapters, many riders find it difficult to open the angle between the thigh and torso this much, and thus they struggle to reach this balance point at top of the rise. Less often, we see people going beyond that point, with their upper body leaning back at the top of the rise, and an angle larger than 180° between the front of the thigh and the torso.

Notice that if we had those elastic cords running down the midline of Heather's back and front, they would still be the same length; it is as if her torso is a block that has been levered up to the top of the rise by her thigh muscles. The 'block' has not become deformed in the process. However, the vast majority of riders pull themselves up to the top of the rise by elongating their front and hollowing their back, making the front elastic longer. Changing this pattern usually becomes the rider's first introduction not only to thigh strength, but also to core muscle strength – strength that is also needed by the athletic horse. As you will see later on, this presents most people with a considerable challenge.

The rider who elongates her front in the rise is showing the same bodily use as the horse who pulls himself along with his front legs. For he too then

2.5

2.6

elongates his stomach muscles, elongates the muscles under his chest, elongates the underside of his neck, and lifts his chin. Like the rider, his back hollows, and this makes it impossible for his hind legs to come underneath him and take powerful, athletic steps. The rider might well be tempted to kick more, in the hope of influencing the hind legs, and/or to pull or fiddle his head down. But in either case, she has missed the point, because both ends of the horse come right once *his back* comes right, and this can only happen when the *rider's back* comes right.

Think of the horse like a strung archery bow, in which the stomach muscles are the string and the back is the wood. **(Fig. 2.4)** It is the shortened stomach muscles that pull the back up, and without the sagging stomach, room is created for the hind legs to step under. Thus the athletic horse and rider are both doing something reminiscent of an abdominal crunch, keeping their stomachs short. Poor human and poor equine movement have the same basis, as do high quality movement. Both horse and rider have to discover how to push themselves along (or up) along from their backside and hind legs, instead of pulling themselves along (or up) with their abdominal muscles and front legs (arms). Rising trot is a fantastic place for the rider to discover how her correct body use influences the horse's muscular use, for when either one of them hollows the other will instinctively follow suit. Conversely, the rider who refuses to hollow her back can make it (quite literally) impossible for the horse to hollow his. Heather makes her part in the maintenance of a correct body pattern look easy but, believe me, it is not.

Most people who first learn to do a correct rising trot mechanism are shocked, not only by the change in the use of their thigh and stomach muscles, and the lack of weight in their stirrups, but also by the size of the rise, and the thrust it requires. They have been taught to keep it small and 'tidy'. But it makes intuitive sense that the rider's thrust should match the thrust of the horse's hind leg; she is then dynamically in balance with him, keeping up with him and not falling in front or behind him. If you watch the training videos/DVDs

**Fig. 2.4**
The hollow-backed horse and the horse in carriage can be compared to an archery bow that is either unstrung (a), or strung (b). In the strung bow of (b), the shortened string pulls the wood into an arc, just as the shortened stomach muscles pull the horse's back into an arc. The muscles of the crest are also involved in this change.

a

b

of any of the top competitive dressage riders, you will see that they all show this mechanism.

However, a pupil of mine recently recounted watching one of them teaching a lesson and telling the rider to make the rise smaller. When the desired change did not materialise, the trainer got on the horse to demonstrate, and she showed a correct mechanism with a big thrust that reached the balance point. 'Do it like this,' she said. My pupil immediately saw the discrepancy, but the rider was left in a double bind. She was witnessing a powerful movement that her teacher defined as 'nothing' – so what felt right to the teacher did not match the look she was attempting to create in her pupil (oh, for a video camera!). Sadly, this disconnection between the wordscape and the brainscape prevented the pupil from finding the right feeling.

In the sit which is shown in **Photo 2.5**, Heather's body is inclined slightly forward, as you also see in the half-way position of **Photo 2.6**. If you do rising trot from an upright sit to an upright rise, you will topple backwards and be unable to control your descent. While some riders do attempt this, others lean too far forward, as you will see. In short, there are many variations on the theme of rising trot, all of which render the rider more or less dysfunctional. Even if she is not actually causing the horse to hollow his back, she becomes unable to cause him to round it, for she does not set a correct framework or template with her body that he has to follow. Beneath that upper echelon of really skilled riders, one does not often see rising trot done well, and you can bet that anyone who condemns it as a waste of time does not have good enough mechanics to have discovered how useful and powerful it can be.

## Sitting trot

**Photo 2.7** (overleaf) shows Heather in sitting trot on the left rein. In contrast to the photograph of the 'sit' in rising trot, it is clear that her upper body is now vertical. As in walk, she has the vertical shoulder/hip/heel line, and would land on the riding arena on her feet if we took her horse out from under her by magic. She also shows the ideal of a straight line from her elbow to her hand and the horse's mouth. One of her most significant defaults shows clearly here, with her head too far in advance of her shoulders. Ideally, she would not be looking down.

In **Photo 2.8** (also overleaf) she shows the more photogenic moment of the 'up'. There is no point in the stride where we would see Heather's backside leave the saddle, and neither would we see the mid-section of her back move. (This is also true when she sits on the massive up–down of passage, as we will see in Chapter 11.) As a young trainee instructor, I cultivated my 'wiggle in the middle', and was told that this was *the* way to sit. It is indeed one way to stop yourself from bouncing; but it is not what you see top-class riders doing, and it does not give the rider much influence. The lumbar spine (between the top of the pelvis and the bottom of the ribs) is not designed to be used in this way, and

**Photos 2.7 and 2.8**
Otto is maximally down in Photo 2.7, and maximally up in Photo 2.8, but in sitting trot Heather does not appear to move. She maintains that shoulder/hip/heel vertical line, her backside does not leave the saddle, and there is no 'wiggle in the middle'.

it is not good for your long-term health to keep sending a wave up your spine that is, in effect, a whiplash. When the rest of the rider's body locks rigid, that whiplash can show as a nodding of the head on the neck. The answer is to absorb the up–down of the horse's movement not in the neck or the lumbar spine, but in the hip, knee and ankle joints. Of these, by far the most important is the hip joint.

This means that sitting trot is like a miniature version of rising trot, except that now, the change in angle makes the rider's torso vertical on the 'down' and slightly behind vertical on the 'up'. (See **Fig. 2.5**) It is a change of only a few degrees (which we cannot see in **Photo 2.7** and **2.8**), but riders vary between not being able to make it happen at all – which results in their backside literally leaving the saddle – and not being able to limit the movement – which results in all sorts of extraneous movements they did not intend to make. It is helpful to think of the rider like one of those wooden puppets that has a small metal ring forming the joints of the ankle, knee and hip, and the wrist, elbow and shoulder. Between the joints the puppet does not give; in fact, it is rigid – a word that will doubtless upset some readers. However, I would contend that skilled riders literally do hold the lumbar spine rigid, as well as creating the effect of rigid thighs, rigid calves, and rigid feet, which provide firm links between movable joints. Contrast this with a rag doll, which can give anywhere, and with many riders, it is as if the bones themselves are rubbery. More riders are like rag dolls than are rigid in their joints as well as their bones, and if, as a rider, you feel as if parts of your body wobble around with a life of their own, you too have a 'rag doll' problem.

a        b

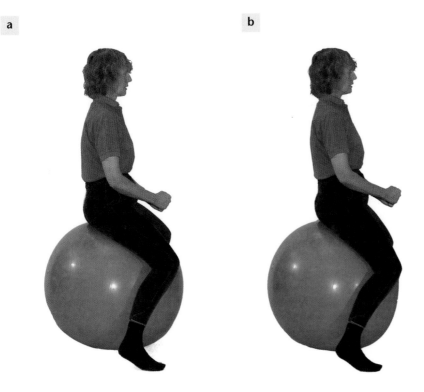

Fig. 2.5
Using a gym ball to demonstrate the 'down' (a) and the 'up' (b) of sitting trot. On the 'up' the hip joint opens to bring the thigh a little closer to vertical, and the upper body slightly back, opening the angle between the thigh and the torso (i.e. opening the angle of the hip joint). On the 'down' the torso comes to vertical and the thigh comes a little more horizontal as the hip angle closes.

What the photographs really cannot tell you is what it takes to not be a rag doll on a horse. Heather is in control of her body from head to toe, back to front, and side to side – and our work together keeps refining this, making subtle changes that give her more control of herself and thus more control of her horses. She makes having this control look easy and natural; but to organise your body in the face of the forces that the horse's movement exerts upon it requires enormous isometric muscle strength (which I will define very soon). This is the exact opposite of the relaxation that most riders aspire to. As I look at the photographs, I see that strength in the quality of Heather's body; most observers, however, would conclude that she is relaxed. This is an assumption which sends them looking in completely the wrong place for answers to the puzzle posed by riding, and I look forward to the day when the horse world as a whole understands the way in which muscles have to *firm up* to create stability.

It is during teacher training courses that I train people to see this. My pupils and I watch riders working and ask ourselves, 'If this rider's skin was a bag, what would be inside it?' The answer can vary from sticks, to feathers, to jelly (or jello in the USA), to bread dough, polystyrene beads, or lead weights … with different qualities in different parts of the body. We do not usually observe each other (either on or off horses) in such an intimate, personal, and perhaps derogatory way. Thus, as a culture, we miss the vital information that comes close to defining skilled riding.

The ideal texture is somewhere near putty, and Heather shows this beautifully throughout her body. Part of her talent is that this has come so easily to her. She is a tall, strong woman and a natural athlete. I, on the other hand, am a midget with naturally low tone, and from a starting point of jelly-like muscles and rather locked joints I have struggled my way to putty-like muscles and much freer joints. (The joints often seize up when muscle tone is low, for as an expression of its inherent instability and weakness, the body 'clutches'.) But that learning process has allowed me to delineate high muscle tone as a key component of skilled riding; those who have it naturally do not know what they have, and do not understand why others cannot 'just sit there' as they do.

To understand this more clearly put your hands out in front of you in a riding position and, while either standing or sitting, push your knuckles against a resistance (**Fig. 2.6**). A wall, the edge of a table, or a partner's hands will do nicely. Keep doing that for a minute or two, and feel what happens to the front of your torso. Somewhere along the midline that joins your pubic bone to your collar bone, you should feel the muscles firm up. See if you can extend the feeling of firmness both up and down, ideally to encompass your whole midline. You are now feeling high isometric muscle tone in the muscles of your front. This makes the muscles bulk out, but not shorten.

This exercise has profound implications. For just as you pushed your hands against a resistance to generate this strength in your front, so having this strength enables Heather to keep pushing her hands forward, as if against an

**Fig. 2.6**
Ideally with a partner, or using the edge of a table or a wall, put your body and hands in a riding position either with your feet level, or with one advanced as shown. Then (in a spirit of co-operation rather than competition) push your hands against each other's resistance. Feel how your abdominal muscles firm up, just as they need to while riding. You can also do this exercise sitting at a desk.

imaginary resistance. This means that it is the key to an 'independent seat'. The front of the body is just one aspect of that strength, and I use a variety of exercises like this to help people find its equivalent in their backs, their sides, their thighs and their calves. All of the exercises involve pushing against a resistance, as it is this which causes the muscles to firm up but not shorten. This is the definition of isometric muscle use, as opposed to isotonic use in which the muscles shorten to move our joints. The latter is much more familiar to us since it generates movement; but the former is the key to good riding, and it generates a particular kind of strength that you will not get from going to the gym.

To generate stability a skilled rider pits opposing muscle groups against each other. As an example of this, put the palms of your hands against each other in a prayer position, and then press them together. In a similar way, the muscles of Heather's front are pitted against those of her back (to keep her vertical, and keep those imaginary elastic cords the same length); she pits her right side against her left side (without which she would almost certainly collapse to one side); she pits the front of the thigh against the underside of the thigh (supporting her own body weight as she 'kneels' as if on an ergonomic stool). She pits the inside of the thigh against the outside of the thigh (taking any possible 'wobble' out of the thighs), and the various aspects of the calf, too, are pitted against each other (for without this, the lower legs will wiggle about with a life of their own).

So Heather is *not* relaxed, and all of these photographs show isometric muscle tone in action. Our horses need us to sit like this, for if we wibble-wobble, how are they supposed to know which movements are intentional –

and therefore classify as aids – and which are unintentional? How can we hope to organise their bodies if we cannot organise our own? How can we possibly imagine that our way of sitting is irrelevant, and does not need to be worked on? Anyone who assumes this has not discovered how exquisitely sensitive horses are to the position and stability of our centre of gravity, how they are affected by our asymmetry, and how – if we want them to respond like athletes – they need us to organise our bodies in a way that makes it possible for us to stop pulling on the reins. So many of the evasions that we blame on them are contortions created in response to the way in which we sit, and I know no end to the subtlety with which – as we peel away the layers of the onion – improvement in our own stability will lead to improvements in their way of going.

The bottom line is that the demands of riding, as a skill, are similar to those of skiing, surfing, wind-surfing (although here you get to hold on to something), snow-boarding, skate-boarding, luge, and bobsled. All of the fit, young athletes who excel at those sports have mastered the art of stabilising themselves on top of a moving and possibly unpredictable medium (which, unlike ours, does not have a mind of its own). They all have high isometric muscle tone, pitting opposing muscle groups against each other. They are certainly not 'uptight'; but they are not relaxed either.

Since snow, wind, and waves do not respond to training, these sports are less shrouded in confusion. Within the riding culture we look too much at the horse, and not enough at the rider. We are blinded by the ideals of the various disciplines, and by the fact that a skilled rider can train a horse to respond to her good bodily use by becoming more athletic, responsive, and 'ridable'. We tacitly ignore the fact that unskilled riding will 'untrain' it significantly faster (after all, this knowledge would not be good for business).

## Canter

**Photos 2.9, 2.10, 2.11** and **2.12** show Heather in canter. They were not all taken in the same canter stride, but **Photo 2.9** shows the first beat of the stride in which the horse's weight is taken solely by his outside hind leg. In **Photo 2.10** this has been joined by the diagonal pair of the inside hind and outside fore, which form the second beat of the canter. In the next photo, only the inside foreleg is on the ground, showing us the third beat. This is followed by the suspension phase of **Photo 2.12**. The outside hind then forms the first beat of the next canter stride, to be joined by the diagonal pair as the second beat, and the inside foreleg as the third.

In trot, the horse's body goes up and down while remaining level. In canter, there is not only an up and down movement, but also a rock in which the quarters lower in the first beat of the stride, and the forehand lowers in the third beat. When the horse is on his forehand, there is less 'sit down' behind and what can feel like a huge 'dive down' in front. Here we have a much more collected canter, which shows more sit down and less dive down. The horse will

not roll over that leading foreleg and bring it behind the vertical; instead he will bend the knee just after the moment shown in **Photo 2.11**, and pick up his foot earlier than a green horse would. As we see in **Photo 2.12** this lifts the whole forehand in preparation for the next stride.

This reduced rock makes it easier for the rider to sit well, and this is just one example of a principle that underlies the whole of riding: *the art of riding lies in making the horse easy to ride*. It is a devastating 'catch 22' that until the rider sits right, the horse will not go right; but until the horse goes right, the rider cannot sit right. Many trainers attempt to help their less skilled pupils work through this by using draw reins to create some semblance of 'right' in the horse, in the hope that this will help the rider to ride well. However, if we force down the head of a hollow-backed horse we force him into a contortion, and give the rider a distorted sense of what 'right' feels like. My own preference is to enter

**Photos 2.9–2.12**
The first, second and third beats of canter, and the moment of suspension. Heather's backside does not leave the saddle, and her shoulders rock slightly forward in the second beat of the stride. Some riders rock forward more than this, some rock back on the third beat, and some bump.

the chicken-and-egg scenario from the other end, using my knowledge of bio-mechanics to create more rightness in the rider, so that this creates more rightness in the horse, which in turn makes it easier for the rider, who thus makes it easier for the horse ... This creates what I call the 'spiral of increasing ease', and the virtuous circle that underlies the ideal of good training.

The rocking movement of canter creates a rock in the rider's upper body. In **Photo 2.10**, Heather's shoulders are ahead of vertical, but in each of the other frames she is dead on vertical. A good quality canter makes it easier to rock less, and also easier to keep the back of your backside in the saddle. Most riders find that, despite their best intentions, it peels up away from the saddle making them bump. In the moment of suspension when the front of the horse moves up, they go up with the horse; but then, when he starts coming down with his quarters, their momentum keeps on sending them up. Thus they come down late. (See **Fig. 2.7**) One of the secrets of good sitting – in both trot and canter – is the ability to turn up into down. Gravity alone is not enough; the rider has, quite literally, to *pull* herself down with the muscles of her ribs, abdomen and back.

This means that many riders do not have their backside in the saddle when that outside hind leg hits the ground (as shown in **Photo 2.9**), and they are far less able to influence it. Heather's backside does not leave the saddle in canter, even while riding greener horses, and it is significant that the rock of her upper body goes predominantly from vertical to forward rather than from vertical to back. Later lessons will show some contrasts to this, and the price that is paid by the rider for a big rock backwards.

In most books on riding, and in the monthly magazines, the implication is that you just look at the pictures of good riders, follow a few instructions, imagine yourself riding like that, and 'presto', off you go. In reality, nobody ever does that unless they are already riding at a level very similar to the model, and for everyone else, it is nowhere near that simple. It takes more than good intentions to help you get control of your body, and furthermore, you cannot change your body mechanics without feeling disorientated, confused, and – to use my favourite word – weird.

To state the obvious, it is not given to all of us to reach the elite levels of our

**Fig. 2.7**
When the rider bumps in either canter or trot, she goes up with the horse, but her momentum keeps sending her up even after he has begun to come down. So she flies off the top of him, and comes down late. She then meets him on the next 'up', and is taken up by him again, only to fly off the top of him ...

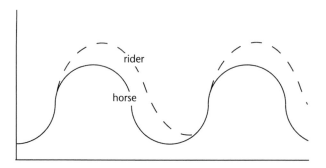

sport. But this for me is not the point. The point is to ride our horses in a more ethical, horse-friendly way, whether or not we wish to be competitive, and regardless of the level at which we compete. It is to become more organised and coherent riders, who make sense to horses by using our bodies to say it in the language 'horse'. To make you think about how your horse might experience you, think about how you experience different people's handshakes – from the limp to the crushing – and how much a handshake tells you about that person. Then imagine how your 'bumshake' (although I prefer to talk of your 'bumprint') might be experienced by your horse, and what you have unwittingly told him about yourself – even before he starts moving. Not many people deliberately change their handshake; but I hope that this book will encourage you to work on your 'bumshake', and make it more horse-friendly.

My hope for each of us is that within our current level of skill and experience, we do our utmost not to inflict a disorganised body upon our horses. Instead of unknowingly perpetuating the problems which we tend to blame on them, we seek to discover how correct biomechanics can show us (and them) the solution to those problems. The point as well is to take each successive next step as we peel away those layers of the onion, and to learn their lessons, enjoying the journey instead of longing to 'arrive'. Riding teaches us about commitment, dedication, sweat, and focus. We learn to 'be in the moment', to become more perceptive, to set ourselves realistic challenges, and to be patient. We learn to work our horses ethically, to enjoy our relationship with them, and to make it possible for them enjoy their relationship with us. If intelligence is defined as 'the ability to respond', then both we and they can become more intelligent. Ideally, too, we appreciate the broader insights that each of these learnings can offer us into life, learning, and even love. Winston Churchill had only glimpsed a very small part of what horses can teach us when he so succinctly said that, 'There is something about the outside of a horse that is good for the inside of a man.'

If some type of virtual-reality experience could enable you to step into Heather's body and experience the muscular work and co-ordinations that make her look as relaxed as most people would presume, you would be astounded (unless you are already an unusually skilled and talented rider). In reality, even the first few steps of the change from your biomechanics to hers will shock you. Given that we have all grown up trying to make sense of phrases like 'relax', 'sit deep', 'use your back' and 'drive him forward', you are almost bound to be labouring under a number of misconceptions. Since high muscle tone is the hidden, unacknowledged dimension of skilled riding, this alone is enough to require a massive about-turn, requiring you to travel in a direction *opposite* to the one you had anticipated.

What is more, even if we lived in some ideal universe where you could read this book and teach yourself to ride at Heather's level of sophistication, it would take you far longer than you might expect. Sport England, in their approach to long-term athlete development, suggest that any elite athlete can only reach that level by practising for about three hours a day, six days a week, for ten years (and Heather has done far more than this in the time that I have known her). This is about a thousand hours a year for ten years, and those ten thousand hours must be spent practising co-ordinations that are as close as possible to those that you and the horse actually need to ingrain, and not some imprecise variation on the theme.* That means that you would spend a minimal amount of time riding your horse overbent, with him running away and crooked to the right, etc., and while we all know that perfection is a mythical ideal that none of us can maintain, you would be required to maintain it far more than most.

Yet in my attempt to be realistic, I am perhaps being pessimistic, for a number of people have proved that it is humanly possible to learn to ride well using my existing books and videotapes/DVDs. A small percentage of the people I have met have done a remarkably good job using only those tools. Many others have, by their own testimonial, improved considerably from their starting point – although when I looked at them for the first time it was clear that they had missed or misdiagnosed some significant factors. Rarely had they made adequately any of the corrections they needed. Doing them to perhaps only ten or twenty per cent of what was needed had made them feel weird enough (so they thought), and they had gone no further. In reality, they had barely glimpsed the changes they needed to make – even though it was simultaneously true that they had improved significantly.

The next four chapters of this book look at riders who demonstrate the four most common 'defaults' as their starting point, and they will, I hope, begin to provide a 'map' that will guide you – as long as you can correctly define your own starting point. There are dangers in this, however. Many avid readers of the original *Masterclass* book have told me that they read it thinking, 'This is me!', and 'This is me too!' and 'I can relate to this problem … and also to this one!', until they felt like someone reading a medical text and discovering that they have all the diseases it describes! I hope this will not happen to you while reading this book, and that you can identify the riders who are not so like you as well as the ones who *are*.

After describing the four most common defaults, the next two lessons look at basic asymmetries, and then we have two case studies that follow the progress of two riders over time. I have worked with Page and Denise for over fifteen years, sharing their struggles in riding a number of horses, and seeing how they have changed, how they have learned new skills and new attitudes, and how, despite it all, they have also stayed the same. These chapters expand the concepts of biomechanics to include lateral work. Then our final chapter, which again shows Heather, gives us a brief look at the 'icing on the cake' of piaffe, passage and pirouettes. The vast majority of readers will not aspire to these; but

---

* The idea of the rider needing ten thousand repetitions of a new co-ordination to progress from 'conscious competence' to 'unconscious competence' was passed on to me via, I suspect, a misunderstanding of the above. Nonetheless, I keep using the idea in my teaching as it provides a useful way to suggest how much commitment will be needed to change a habit!

they have lessons to teach us that – yet again – illuminate the basics.

On the first course when I taught Heather, we all went out for a meal one evening, and I was very moved as she proposed a toast to me as her teacher and mentor. At that time I had no idea where our friendship would lead; but nonetheless, I was so moved that I found myself surreptitiously wiping away a tear as everyone raised their glasses. But my emotions were swept into laughter as Lesley – whose vision began our story – chose that pause with glasses raised to add, 'And may all your rides be weird!'

Within the community of riders and coaches who form many of my friends, this has become a toast, a way of thinking, and a way to chuckle about the difficulties we all face in learning. For the answers always come from somewhere 'out of the box'. So may this book shake you out of the 'sameness' in which you always do what you always did and always get what you always got. May it propel you off your plateau – out of your complacency, your confusion, or your angst – and introduce you to the thrills and spills of the learning process. May you discover the way that learning involves change, and change involves 'strange', giving all new feelings an element of surprise. In short, 'May all your rides be weird!'

# PART 2

# THE CLINIC

The previous chapter took you into the rarified world of an elite rider… welcome back to the real world of everyday riders, who are struggling to master the basics that enable them to organise their bodies and ride their horses in carriage….

**The four defaults**
Tipping forward
Hollowing the back
Rounding the back
Leaning back

**Asymmetries**
Symmetry and the turning aids
Stacking the torso

**Building the skills**
Focused concentration
Lateral work
Advanced work: half-pass, piaffe, passage and pirouettes

# THE FOUR DEFAULTS

**Tipping forward** · Chapter 3

**Hollowing the back** · Chapter 4

**Rounding the back** · Chapter 5

**Leaning back** · Chapter 6

# Tipping forward | Carol

I FIRST MET CAROL TWO years ago, when she contrived to attend a clinic in Maryland, stopping off during the journey that transported her new horse from North Carolina to her home near Boston. She had literally only ridden him pre-purchase, and when she arrived at the clinic I think she was horrified by the reality of a situation that had seemed so ideal on paper! She did well, especially given that her previous experience solely involved show jumping. But because of the expense of travelling him, this was the only time she has ridden that horse with me. She has, however, shown up in a few unexpected places during my travels, and ridden a school horse or a friend's horse, so this is her fourth three-day clinic.

Here we see her riding Arthur, a seven-year-old 15.2hh warmblood by Gaugin de Lully, bred by Page (see Chapter 9) who organised the clinic. He has had some basic dressage training but really has more talent for jumping, and Page plans to sell him as a jumper. Carol had ridden him in a similar clinic three months prior to this, so it was not their first encounter. She readily admits to having a nervous disposition, and at the beginning of the lesson, the combination of having to contend with Arthur, myself, and the camera, sent her flying into the grips of her old default. The calm inner voice that should have been reminding her to breathe deeply and realign herself had left the scene, and **Photo 3.1** shows her tipped forward. She has closed what I call 'the front angle' between her thigh and torso, and she sits with her seat bones pointed back. She shows this default to an extreme – it is her fatal flaw.

By conventional wisdom, tipping forward should be so easy to correct: you just lean back more! On one level this is true, but it fails to recognise the origins of the problem. Years of jumping training have reinforced this position, but also, Carol's nerves make her feel safer when her body is closer to the horse's neck. While her logical brain tells her that this is not the case, her instinct wins in times of stress. But more importantly, the flexor muscles at the front of her body are shorter and stronger than the extensor muscles at the back. So if the

**Photo 3.1**
At the start of Carol's lesson she is tipped forward, whilst Arthur has hollowed his back and is admiring the view.

rider's spine were a flexible mast held up by guy ropes, the shortened front guy ropes would keep pulling it forward. (We will meet a number of riders whose guy ropes cause various distortions; needless to say, Heather's are so well balanced that it is easy for her to sit in neutral spine.) For Carol, leaning forward is 'home', and like most people with this problem, she has always slept on her side, curled into a foetal position. That eight hours a night creates a powerful imprint in the body, and neither willpower nor obedience are strong enough tools to counter it.

In **Photo 3.2** Arthur's supporting pair of legs are not yet vertical, so they have not reached the moment which defines the top of the rise. Here, we would hope to see Carol with that knee-to-hip-to-shoulder vertical line. But she is so tipped forward that she cannot possibly get the front angle to open enough to reach that point (although she did manage this later, as you will see in **Photo 3.9**). Furthermore, if we took her horse out from under her by magic, she would not land on the riding arena on her feet. Her lower leg is so far forward that, despite her shoulders being forward, she would still topple back onto her backside.

Arthur is above the bit, happily admiring the view. Like all horses and riders, he and Carol are mired in the 'catch 22' that underlies the whole of riding: for until she sits right he cannot go right, but until he goes right she cannot sit right. At this point in time he is *pushing back* at her. It is as if someone had put her hand on his muzzle and scrunched his muzzle back into his poll, his poll back into his neck, his neck back into his wither, and his wither back into his back, creating the hollow of the 'man-trap'. The more Carol's shoulders come forward, the more her backside slides backwards down into that hollow. Without even realising, she has colluded with him. Her default is one of the four possible ways in which riders fall back into the 'man-trap'.

**Photo 3.2**
In rising trot, Carol's feet are so far forward and her torso is so tipped forward that she cannot possibly reach the balance point at the top of the rise.

I soon bought Carol to halt, for while she is in movement I have little chance of changing her patterns, and only by putting my hands on her can I speak directly to her body. This gives my intervention much more power. My aim is to give her a 'reference feeling', which we will then attempt to maintain in motion. In reality, Carol has been through this process before, and I am bringing her back to a place that I hope she will recognise.

People vary enormously in how well they retain the input they have been given in a clinic. Riding a different horse and being over-awed by the situation threw Carol out of kilter in this moment, but, as I remember, she reported feeling rather lost in her riding at home. She might, of course, have been doing better than she had thought – although more often the reverse is true and riders think they are doing quite well when actually they are losing it. What was once a clear sense of 'right' can slip through the rider's fingers (and away from her backside) without her even realising. One of my most important aims is to teach the rider to 'read' the horse's language, so that she starts to recognise the way that her horse is continually giving her feedback. The extremes of getting it and losing it are normally very obvious, but those shades of grey in the middle take quite some skill to decipher.

My intention is that people leave a clinic with a 'recipe' for the changes they need to make. (Instead of having a magnificent ride that was a one-off experience, I would rather they left with smaller changes that are reproducible.) But over time they tend to distort that recipe, using too much of one ingredient and too little of another, and thus they, as well as the horse, will stray from the straight and narrow. In fact, it is probably the *rider* who disorganises the horse rather than the horse who disorganises the rider; but either way, they soon need outside help to get back on track. The first half of the first lesson of their next

**Photo 3.3**
Carol has lifted her legs up over the front of the saddle, and I am running my hand down her back to help her find neutral spine.

**Photo 3.4**
As I bring Carol's leg back into place, I make sure that her inner thigh muscle is rotated towards the back.

**Photo 3.5**
I then check that the ball of her foot is resting lightly in the stirrup, and that she now has a vertical shoulder/hip/heel line.

clinic usually sees this happening, and as riders put two and two together, they often start muttering 'Now I get it …', 'How stupid of me …'. With that baseline reaffirmed, they hopefully become ready for more input.

So **Photos 3.3**, **3.4** and **3.5** show a sequence that begins with me lifting Carol's legs up over the front of the saddle. It is safest to do this with the feet still in the stirrups, and with someone holding the horse. In this position it is easier for the rider to find 'neutral spine', and in **Photo 3.3** I am running my hand down Carol's back, and manoeuvring her gently into the place where I feel just a slight forward curve in the small of her back. Whenever I do this, I might also ask the rider, 'Can you feel your seat bones?' and 'Would they point down to the ground, towards the horse's front feet, or towards his hind feet?' Once they are pointing straight down, we have our first approximation to neutral spine. Then, as I bring the rider's legs back down into place, I want her to keep that same orientation.

**Photo 3.4** shows me rotating the muscle of Carol's inside thigh around to the back as I bring her leg back into place. This inward rotation brings the thigh bone itself closer to the saddle, which in turn brings the knee more onto it and the toe more in. This comes as a shock to the many people who have been trying to 'relax their thigh and take their knee off the saddle'. When I have positioned the thigh I check that the stirrup is on the ball of the foot, with the foot resting lightly in it, as in **Photo 3.5**. I then stand back, to double-check the shoulder/hip/heel line, and to be sure that the rider still has neutral spine.

When I ask the rider, 'What does this feel like compared to normal?' her words will set the tone for the rest of the lesson. She might feel that her feet are more back and her thighs rotated in, with a stretch down the front or inside of them. She might feel (as in Carol's case) that she is leaning back, or that she is slouched, or tall, or forward. The most important factor is that these words link her brainscape to her wordscape, flagging the change that the rider needs to make, and giving it a label. Some people process information more through images than through direct body awareness, and if a rider wishes to tell me that she feels like Quasimodo, or like frozen cheese, so be it. The words themselves are not important; what is important is that they form a label that the rider will not confuse with any other possible co-ordination, as she might if we were using my words. Her words will lead us directly to the right feeling.

While the rider's words will always have the most meaning for her (even if they do not do much for me), we need to have some standardised language so that large groups of people attach the same feeling to the same words and can understand each other. Thus the next most important ingredient I called 'bearing down', and this use of the abdominal muscles separates talented riders from those who struggle. When I first met Heather she did it naturally, albeit in a way that was compromised by her original default, and she has refined bearing down in many ways since. It was a discovery that I made by chance twenty-eight years ago, and it changed my life dramatically. I also know from pupils, colleagues, and from the many letters I receive, that I am not the only person to have found it life-changing. In **Photo 3.6** my hands are on Carol's front and back, just below the level of her sternum, and I have asked her to clear her throat. This, along with coughing, sneezing, and giggling, makes you bear down naturally. The best linguistic description I have found is that you pull your stomach in to make the muscles into a wall, and then push your guts against that wall. I sometimes wish I had called it 'bear out' instead of 'bear down', for this misleads some people into thinking that they should push their weight down harder into the saddle. When bearing down the body does not become heavier, but it does become more stable.

At the level of the lumbar spine between the ribs and hips, the push goes in all directions, hence I have a hand on Carol's back as well as on her abdomen, and I am pressing inwards, increasing the strength of the wall that she has to push her guts against. I followed this by putting my hands on her sides, testing the push in that direction too. I then put my fingers lower down as shown in **Photo 3.7** to test the strength of her bear down at this level. Here, the pelvis is like three sides of a bony box, so the 'push' is only felt in the soft tissue at the front.

Putting my hands on Carol's body is an important strategy that

**Photo 3.6**
I have my hands on the back and front of Carol's waist, giving her a resistance to push against as she learns to bear down, and making sure that she attaches the right feeling to my words.

**Photo 3.7**
With my hand on Carol's lower stomach I check the strength and quality of her 'low down bear down'.

3.6    3.7

I use to reduce any possible 'slippage' between the feeling I mean by those words and the feeling the rider attaches to them. Misunderstandings like this have contaminated phrases like 'sit deep' and 'use your back', as well as the word 'push'. These words almost always go unquestioned in the riding arena, and for many riders they are just phrases in the wordscape. Other riders attach them to any one of the many possible feelings they can conjure up in the brainscape. Like a huge multi-generational game of 'Telephone' or 'Chinese Whispers', these phrases have evolved over the years to have a meaning quite different to the meaning their originator meant to convey. 'Push' might even mean 'bear down', i.e. push your guts against the wall of your stomach muscles. However, most riders assume that it instructs you to push your backside around in the saddle.

Whenever you sweep the yard by pushing a broom away from you, you utilise the power of bearing down. This is the implicit knowledge of a talented sweeper; but next time you sweep, pay attention, and notice explicitly what you are doing. I often show a large audience the power of bearing down by asking one audience member to teach the others how to blow their nose. I suggest that the audience are not actually humans, but are Martians, sent as the advance party to colonise planet Earth. Martians are very literal creatures who follow all instructions to the letter of the law, without any improvisation. So my stooge usually gives very precise instructions about fingers, tissues and nostrils, while leaving out the most important point: the power to blow your nose comes from your stomach muscles. Without this, there will not be much in your tissue to show for your efforts (try it!).

That same power is harnessed by martial artists, and by tennis players. The hardest hitters are the loudest grunters, who use that grunt to increase the power they can transmit from their core to their racket. Although it does not involve movement, bearing down while riding is like pedalling a bicycle as opposed to free wheeling. Again it provides power, and if you watch beginners on a trail ride it is clear that they sit in a way that is *inactive* rather than *proactive*. They provide an extreme example, but very few riders bear down to the extent that enables them to push their hands forward as Heather does. Remember the exercise in Chapter 2 (page 45, **Fig. 2.6**) in which pushing your hands forward against a resistance automatically makes you build a strong wall in your stomach muscles and push your guts against it. This is a very good way to access bearing down.

Yet another way to discover its value is to sit on a firmly blown-up gym ball in an 'on horse' position with your feet on the ground, and have a friend attempt to destabilise you. She can push with gradually increasing firmness on your upper chest or upper back (no sudden movements and no rough-housing!), and can also use a sideways push on either shoulder, and pushes on your waist. In another variation on the theme, she can attempt to roll the ball out from under you in various directions (again, begin cautiously). You will no doubt find that you are more stable in response to some pushes than you are in

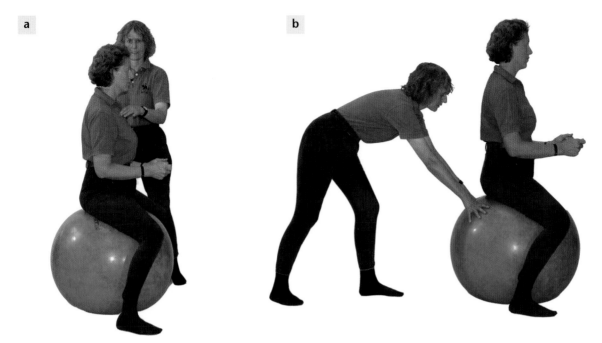

response to others, and that bearing down lies at the heart – or the core – of your response. Also, this exercise may help you to recognise your own default way of falling down into the 'man-trap'. Do you tend to be round-backed or hollow-backed? To topple forwards or backwards? (See **Fig.3.1**)

In **Photo 3.8** Carol is walking on again, and as well as looking much more lined up she is much more emotionally settled. Her heel is well above her toe, but in the overall scheme of things, I can live with this when she has made such a good job of changing so much. Part of my art lies in deciding both what to say

**Fig. 3.1**
(a) As the rider sits on a gym ball in an 'on-horse' position with her feet on the floor, I can use a gradually increasing resistance to test her stability.
(b) As I attempt to roll the gym ball out from under the rider, she has to stabilise herself to resist its movement.

**Photo 3.8**
Here in walk Carol is much more lined up. She has changed the organisation of her torso, thigh and calf and is barely tipped forward, although her heel is up.

and what to *not* say, for we all have limits on our available 'brainspace'. Other professionals are often surprised by my choices, which do not have the same priorities as conventional wisdom; but I think we can all agree that no one can change everything all at once. There is no choice but to peel that onion layer by layer, and I want to give each rider the most 'bang for her buck', helping her to home in on causes rather than symptoms. I want to make the changes that will be most beneficial now, while also building a strong base for her future learning.

Once Carol had reached this stage, it was time to remind her about breathing. It is not hard to bear down strongly if you hold your breath, but riders have to breathe at the same time, and most people struggle with this. In fact, many are tempted to sell out on bearing down because they find it so stressful, and find breathing alongside it almost impossible! Also, it seems so contrary to the advice they have been given over years, for when you first learn to bear down, it feels far from 'relaxed'. Essentially, I rely on the rider's feelings of empowerment and her horse's response to sell the idea to her, and over one or two lessons I normally succeed. But I do not always succeed in getting the commitment over time that such a radical change entails. Bearing down can become automatic, natural and easy, even for people who baulked when they first met the idea. It can become like the smell you do not notice any more – and then you too might join the minority of riders who do it automatically but perceive themselves as relaxed!

My recommendation is that riders practise breathing and bearing down off horse, and driving your car provides the perfect opportunity. Bearing down and breathing must become a way of life, for you will not breathe one way twenty-three hours a day and then get on your horse and breathe differently for hour twenty-four. It requires diaphragmatic breathing, which you learn explicitly if you sing or play a wind instrument. I often suggest that riders think of having a chemistry flask inside them, with a long neck leading to a round bowl that is down in their pelvis. (See **Fig. 3.2**) Their aim is to get the air to go all the way down the long neck and into the round bowl. It may help to imagine a pair of bellows inside the bowl, sucking the air down into it. On the out-breath, it can help to think of a little tap on the midline of the body at bikini-line level, and to imagine that the air comes out through that tap. Making the noise 'Pssssht' makes that happen automatically.

Carol needed some reminders about rising-trot mechanism, but the concept is not new to her. **Photo 3.9** shows her at the top of the rise, looking much more like Heather. She has a much more open angle between the thigh and torso, and would now land on the riding arena on her feet if we took her horse out from under her by magic. In **Photo 3.10** the changes in Carol are filtering through to Arthur, who is beginning to reach into the rein. The photograph is taken just after the point in the stride which shows us if he is tracking up, and Carol still has quite good angles, far more open than they were in **Photos 3.1** and **3.2**. By **Photo 3.11** he has really begun to look like a dressage horse, tracking up and

**Fig. 3.2**
It helps riders to imagine a chemistry flask inside them, as if their windpipe were longer than it really is, and they could draw each in-breath right down into the flask.

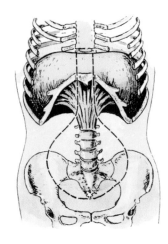

Photo 3.9
Carol can now reach the top of the rise, replicating the mechanics you saw in Heather. She would land on the riding arena on her feet if we took her horse out from under her by magic.

reaching into the rein, although Carol is not so well in balance over her foot as she is in the previous two photographs.

So how did this change in Arthur happen? Initially he was pushing back at Carol, contracting his neck and back to form the hollow of the 'man-trap'. As well as bringing his mouth away from the rein contact and his back away from her weight, he was also contracting his ribcage away from her thighs, and limiting his breathing. These 'cramping reflexes' can put horse and rider into what I call the spiral of increasing tension, since the constrictions in each party's body makes it harder for the other. But Arthur has now begun to show the 'seeking reflexes', and he and Carol have found their way into the spiral of increasing ease. His back has lifted to seek contact with her seat, his neck has reached and arched to seek contact with the rein, and his ribcage has filled out to seek contact with her thigh. As his breathing and movement become much

Photo 3.10
Carol has good biomechanics, and Arthur is beginning to reach into the rein. He is close to tracking up and has his ears out sideways – both good signs.

Photo 3.11
Arthur comes into the seeking reflexes – lifting his back, reaching into the rein, and tracking up. Carol's balance over her foot is not quite so good as it is in Photo 3.10, and Arthur has pricked his ears. These both suggest that her success might be short-lived!

more fluid, so it becomes easier for Carol to ride him well.

During the lesson Carol had to do a huge amount of muscular work to stop her feet and shoulders coming forward, stopping the fold that makes her back-side slide back down the 'man-trap', concentrating her weight there and either making or perpetuating the hollow. Once the horse has provided a 'man-trap' for the rider, the laws of physics are against her, and it is an uphill struggle (quite literally) to counteract the tendency to slide back. Carol has to open the front angle and 'kneel' more, which spreads her weight along the length of her thigh instead of concentrating it in the middle of his back. It is as if somebody pulled her pelvis forward and up, as in limbo dancing, and thus pulled the horse's back up with her; but this somebody has to be her.

Additionally, she has to bear down so strongly that she generates a push forward within her torso that is stronger than Arthur's push back. Quite literally, the push of her bear down pushes his head and neck away from her, and when her push overcomes his, he will join her by reaching his neck forward into the seeking reflexes. Also, the lower arm and rein need to create a contact for him to reach into; if the rein is a loop – as it often was early in the session – there is very little chance that he will indeed reach away. I suggested that Carol thought of the lower arm and the rein forming the walls of a corridor that she wanted to channel him down. The thought 'thighs narrow, hands wide' helped her to keep the inner thigh rotated in and weight bearing, while the hands maintained that corridor. If Arthur contracted his neck and put slack into the rein, her aim was to widen her hands apart to take up that slack, preferably before it ever materialised.

The ideal position for her hands created, as she looked at them, a long narrow triangle from the width of her elbows via the width of her hands to the width of the bit. If she needed to, she could widen her hands from this position, but not narrow them. This effectively blocks the channel though which she aims the push of her bear down. In **Photo 3.9** Carol's hands have come too close together, and in **Photo 3.11** they should also be wider. **Photo 3.8**, taken in walk, shows the corridor most clearly, and her wrists are better organised than they are in the subsequent photographs in trot. In **Photo 3.8** Carol is 'kneeling' well, but the rein has a very slight loop, and the push forward of her bear down is not yet stronger than Arthur's push back. Hence he is not yet reaching into the rein.

Heather's arms formed this same triangle, although what we see most clearly in photographs (and what is emphasised most by teachers) is the straight line that is lost if the hands are too high or low. One of the biggest dangers for Carol is that her reins become too long, either because they slip through her fingers, or because she draws her hands backwards to take up the slack in them. In either case, as she brings her hand back she concurrently closes that front angle, which brings her backside back. So she slides back down into his 'man-trap', re-quiring her to lever herself out of it all over again. This would never happen to Heather, partly because she has a different default, and partly because her body has the strength and stability to hold its rightness even in the face of the horse's wrongness, keeping rightness in her hand position too. Being less reactive makes it so much easier to ride well!

Coupled with bearing down and maintaining the contact, Carol has to get the horse's attention as she has in **Photo 3.10**, where his ears are sideways – although in **Photo 3.11** they are pricked, suggesting that she might be about to lose his brain if not his body. When horses prick their ears their push back doubles, and they make an even bigger 'man-trap'. So it really pays to hold the horse's attention, and this requires you to make yourself more compelling to him than the outside world. The more strongly you bear down and the more still you sit, the more seriously the horse takes you; but you also have to kick whenever he pricks his ears. Better still, you kick *before* he pricks his ears, and as you move your leg from the knee down, nothing must change from the knee up. If you topple backwards (through any of the four defaults) you will lose more than you gain.

Carol has ridden with me enough to know all this in theory, and the challenge is to make it work in practice. During this lesson I said things I had said before, and also made several new suggestions that were particularly helpful to her. I wish I had realised many years ago that anyone whose backside slides back has an underlying issue that works alongside the shortened flexor muscles to hold the problem in place. It concerns the pelvic floor, and is rather personal. So I hope you will forgive me for reporting the direct way in which I asked Carol: 'Would you perceive your underneath from the front towards the back or from the back towards the front?' (You might ask yourself the same question, even as you are sitting in your chair – if you tip forward or are hollow-backed the answer might change your life!) Realise that we are talking here only about *perception*; but this has enormous effects on how we organise our energy and our muscles. As I expected, Carol thought of her underneath from the front towards the back. The pattern of tipping forward will not change until she changes this, and as she struggled to reverse this feel-sense, so she became much more able to consistently overcome her default. Like bearing down and breathing well, this is something that can be practised in everyday life, until it too is automatic, both on and off the horse.

Since we are now talking personally, let me add another particularly helpful idea for those who struggle to make a powerful and effective bear down. Carol was familiar with the thought of 'beginning her bear down in her back', which I will explain in the lesson with Millie (Chapter 5). But it helped her more to think of the push of her bear down beginning in her cervix. For women, this marks the mid-point of the pelvis (and a male friend of mine who teaches Tai Chi bemoans the fact that men have no landmark they can relate to which tells them where their centre is!) Thinking of the muscles and organs deep inside you is very different to thinking just about the muscles of your six-pack and your skin. Again, perception is the key.

Towards the end of the lesson Carol clearly felt the changes you see in **Photo 3.11**, as Arthur's back came up as his neck reached and arched into the rein. This was my aim, and the next two lessons built on this, making the response more repeatable and consistent, taking it into canter, and beginning work on Carol's asymmetry. It is harder for her to keep 'kneeling' and keep those angles open on the right rein, basically because her body rotates to the right. (We tackle this issue in the lesson with Sue in Chapter 7.) But perhaps my most bizarre suggestion during the entire lesson was that she imagined strings of chewing gum from her underneath to the saddle, and that these pulled the saddle and his back up with her in each rise. Remarkable as it may sound, this thought made an immediate difference. It would not have worked without keeping her front angle more open, with weight down through her thigh and power in her bear down. But it added icing to the cake, and was a hit with Carol because 'think it and it happens' requires much less sweat than the other (apparent) contortions she was struggling to make!

My hope is that Carol left this clinic in a more secure state than she was in when she arrived. I have seen many people take between sixteen and twenty-four lessons to begin to have both the tools and the presence of mind to keep returning to their new 'home' without input from a teacher. The trick lies in recognising when you are losing the changes you have made, and knowing what to do about it when you do. Conversely, I meet many people who, at the beginning of their first lesson, tell me that they have always leant forward; but as I watch them they are actually leaning back (although this may change if they panic in canter). Without even realising, they have solved their biggest problem! Their next fix is very much easier, and its biggest issue is the element of surprise. Carol's fatal flaw is as strong as I have seen it in anyone, and I suspect that she will always need to think the thoughts and make the feelings that counteract her tendency to tip forward. I doubt if she will ever over-correct and find herself leaning back too much – if she does, I shall welcome her to the next phase in her learning, and raise a cheer to her persistence and determination!

# CHAPTER 4

# Hollowing the back | Jo

J O IS THE LEAST EXPERIENCED rider featured in this book. She was a pony-mad kid, who rode at a local 'riding school' where, as she remembers it, the instructions were limited to 'hands down', 'heels down', and 'grip with your knees'! Adult life then took her into the worlds of social work and business training, where her experiences led her to become a trainer of neuro-linguistic programming. NLP is often defined as 'the study of the structure of subjective experience', and my own training in the field has hugely influenced the way in which I communicate with riders. It has also shed light on the ways in which we either open ourselves to learning and change, or contrive to stay stuck.

Through NLP Jo discovered 'Thought Field Therapy', and she then trained extensively with its founder Dr Roger Callaghan. TFT is, in my opinion, the state-of-the-art therapy for working with post-traumatic stress. After the troubles in Kosovo it became the treatment of choice of the government there, and Jo was one of the team who travelled out to train their mental health practitioners. She has since specialised in working with riders who want to improve their confidence and/or performance, using her own combination of NLP and TFT (see www. jo-cooper.com). Jo has recently returned to riding after a twenty-year gap, and when she began having lessons she felt disorientated by the changes in even conventional teaching. She was also upset that her childhood skills had deserted her. Now that she is feeling more secure she hopes to fulfil a life-long dream by getting her own horse.

Before we took these photographs Jo had taken one clinic with me. The experiences of her career have made her a good pupil, and since she has not invested a huge amount of time and money in learning to do it wrong, she is more than willing to change. She has less 'baggage' than the other riders who illustrate the defaults, but this advantage is mitigated by the disadvantage of her inexperience. In all of the photographs she looks a bit wobbly, and if she were a stuffed-toy rider she would have much less stuffing than either Heather or Carol. In **Photo 4.1** especially her arms look as if they are not part of her body

– as if she does not yet know what to do with them – and she has little idea of how to find a correct contact on the rein. In fact, the issue for riders at Jo's level is partly about learning good biomechanics, but is also about *rights* – having the right to have an influence, saying to the horse 'Sorry, honey, we are not going to do it that way. Try it like this …'.

Erica is a ten-year-old Welsh pony who is kept with us at livery, and who often works on my courses. Her owner has always been a 'happy hacker', but she now has more interest in riding well, and has been thrilled to find that Erica's way of going has improved since she has been kept with us. However, it would be stretching the truth to say that the pony has had dressage training; she spends most of her time enjoying our beautiful Cotswold bridlepaths with her owner!

**Photo 4.1** shows the right rein in walk, and both Erica and Jo have a hollow back. In trot Jo's hollow becomes even more marked as shown in **Photo 4.2**, and it is clear that Erica cannot come close to tracking up while carrying herself like this. To understand how this works, stand up, and bend your torso forward from your hips, attempting to make your back flat. (I am grateful to equine sports massage therapist Pennie Hooper who devised this exercise.) Then put your hands just above your knees. Imagine that you are a horse, and realise that your knees are the equivalent of the horse's stifles. So, unlike you, his thigh bones lie within his quarters. Look up as you hollow your back, and attempt to walk in this position. (See **Fig. 4.1**) It pushes your knees (the horse's stifles) backwards, and you can barely make your legs move. Even if your rider were to hit you, you could not take bigger steps, and if you were put in draw reins your plight would become even worse. (You can imitate this by keeping your back hollow as you

**Photo 4.1**
Jo begins her lesson looking hollow backed, and with her foot slightly ahead of the ideal shoulder/hip/heel vertical line. She would land on the arena on her backside if we took her horse out from under her by magic.

**Photo 4.2**
In rising trot Jo has hollowed her back and lifted her chest even more. She would now topple forward if her horse were taken out from under her by magic.

**a**

**b**

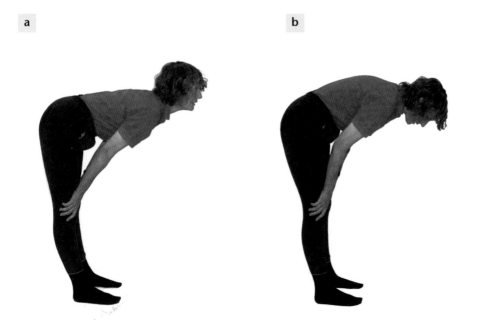

Fig. 4.1
(a) If I imitate a hollow-backed horse by bending forward at the hips, hollowing my back, and looking up, my 'hind legs' can only take very small steps.

(b) Rounding my back and elongating the back of my neck stops my knees (stifles) from being forced backwards, and I can now take much longer steps.

bring your head down – and if you now imagine being hit while being held in this position, you might begin to understand the double-bind this can put the horse into.) But if you round your back in that initial position your knees (stifles) are much less stressed, and you can take far longer steps. You become a much better athlete, as you suddenly have mobility in your knees and hips, and room to bring your hind legs forward under your belly.

Hollow-backed humans have a similar problem with their knees, and if you typically stand with yours pushed backwards and hyper-extended, suspect yourself of being hollow both as you walk and ride. Practise bending your knees a little, and letting your waistband come back. In this default, the rider's seat bones point back as she slides back down the 'man-trap', and while this happens to both Carol and Jo, they each have a different configuration of guy ropes. Carol's short front guy rope closes the angle between her thigh and torso, but Jo's short *back* guy rope contracts her back into that hollow. Then as the rider becomes more practised, Jo's default can evolve into the default illustrated by Diane in Chapter 6. In the more sophisticated version of a hollow back, the rider's backside is less out behind her, but she leans back from her waist. Try moving between both versions as you sit in your chair, and realise that the hollow is still there in each case.

Many riders have dedicated their lives to learning to ride like this, and phrases like 'grow tall' and 'stick your chest out' have misled them (and perhaps their teachers) into perfecting a posture that no martial artist would ever use. The bottom line is that whenever either horse or rider hollows, the other one will almost always follow suit, and the rider has to learn how to take the hollow out of *her own* back before she can convince the horse to do the same.

The other three riders who illustrate the basic defaults are all extreme examples of a type. Jo is less extreme, and also there was a shorter time span between

**Photo 4.3**
This might look tall and elegant, but actually Jo's back is hollow.

the photoshoot and her last lesson, giving her less time to 'lose it'. So when you first look at **Photo 4.3** you might not see anything wrong. But look more closely at the line of her back, and realise that both her back and front make a single forward curve, which is not the shape of 'neutral spine'. (Refer back to **Photo 2.1** and **Fig. 2.3**.) In the posture of **Photo 4.3** Jo, unlike Heather, would have a long elastic cord down the midline of her front, and a short one down her back. She has rolled forward onto her crotch, sitting with her pubic bone too down, her seat bones pointing back, and her chest aiming well above the horse's ears.

If you compare **Photo 4.3** with **Photo 4.4**, the change in Jo's back becomes obvious. Here she has placed her thumb on the 'salt cellar' in the centre of her

**Photo 4.4**
Shows Jo in neutral spine, with her thumb on the centre of her collar bone, and her little finger on her sternum. I, however, am hollowing my back, with my thumb behind (rather than over) my little finger.

collar bone and has reached her little finger down towards her sternum. When the rider sits in neutral spine, her collar bone is over her sternum, which is over her belly button, which is over her pubic bone, so (if we ignore the odd roll of fat) her front forms a straight vertical line. In **Photo 4.3** notice how Jo's collar bone is a long way behind her sternum, while in **Photo 4.4** her torso is much more box-shaped, and her backside has virtually disappeared. Stomachs largely disappear, too, as the rider brings her belly button back and her waistband back, for making those elastics the same length puts her guts back into the bowl of her pelvis. However, **Photo 4.4** also shows me standing with my thumb behind my little finger, and my stomach and backside are all too obvious! In **Photo 4.4** Jo's seat bones point down instead of back, and her chest aims to about where the browband meets the headpiece. However, this will vary according to the relative size of horse and rider, and some people have to aim their chest to the bit rings!

This exercise is a very good way to check yourself, and if your default is to be hollow, you are likely to be very shocked at how slouched you feel, and how down your chest is when your fingers are lined up. You can also check for neutral spine by placing one or both hands under one or both of your seat bones. (You can do this now while sitting in your chair, but I recommend that you also do it in the saddle.) Move slowly between the hollow back that points your seat bones back, and the round back that points them forward. One posture might be much more familiar and easy to get into than the other, and this tells you a lot about your own default. Come to rest in the position that points your seat bones down. Ideally, double-check this by sitting sideways-on to a large mirror, because if your usual 'home' is way off neutral, you might think your seat bones point down when you actually need to make a much bigger change. Your hands will help you to be objective; but notice too if those imaginary elastics *look* the same length when you think that they *feel* the same length.

Some might consider that Jo looks much more elegant in **Photo 4.3** than she does in **Photo 4.4** (although they would probably not quibble about how elegant Heather looks as she shows the same posture in **Photo 4.1**). Hollow-backed riders certainly *feel* more elegant in their default posture than they do in neutral spine, and this is usually their biggest objection to making the single most important change that could revolutionise their riding. There is, however, a secret to becoming elegant while sitting in neutral spine. You pay attention to your armpits, and notice if they are more closed at the front or more closed at the back. They are likely to be more closed at the front, and when you change this (without bringing your collar bone or shoulders back) you suddenly look elegant.

In the horse world, huge confusion surrounds the way in which teachers think about the upper back and shoulders. The upper back can curve forward or back, putting your thumb in front of, over, or behind your sternum when you place your hand as in **Photo 4.4**. In a completely separate articulation, your

**Fig. 4.2**
Riders who slouch, as in (a) are often told to lift their chest, which results in the posture of (b). Their head then has to come forward to counterbalance their shoulders. Closing the armpits at the back, as in (c) is a far better solution to the problem, although the rider may initially find herself gazing at the horse's wither. The final correction that puts her head on top of her shoulders may not be easy for her to make.

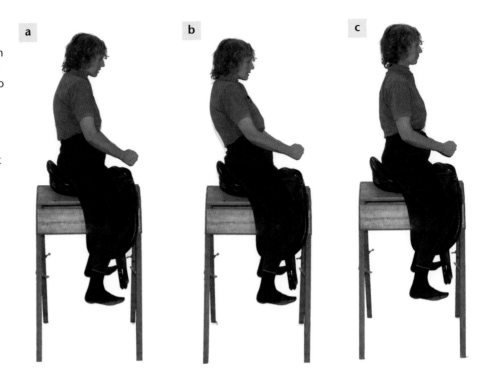

a  b  c

shoulder blades can slide over your ribs, coming closer together or further apart. As they widen, your armpits close at the front and your chest collapses. As you bring your shoulder blades more together your armpits close at the back and you look more elegant. When the pupil's back is rounded it is often because her armpits are closed at the front – but the teacher makes her lift her chest, which is the wrong correction. Then, she is left with her chest lifted, her back hollow, and her armpits closed at the front. (Try it!) Many people stand, walk, and also ride like this, and they only keep their balance by putting their head forward. Their eyes continue to look straight ahead (not up or down), which tricks the body into thinking all is well.

If you start in this position and then close your armpits at the back, the counter-balance of your head becomes more obvious, and the answer is to realign yourself firstly by putting your collar bone over your sternum, and then by closing your armpits at the back. As you do this your head will probably maintain its relationship to your shoulders, so this new posture puts it in advance of your body. If you are riding, this gives you a panoramic view of the horse's wither – you have the same problem you always had, but suddenly you know about it! The final correction (which is the hardest for most people) is to bring your head back over your shoulders.

Next time you are faced with a teacher who demands that you grow tall, stick your chest out, or become more elegant, see if you can earn yourself a 'Good' simply by bringing your collar bone over your sternum and closing your armpits at the back. It is very likely that you can – although, if you too have made a habit of this compensatory strategy, the position of your head may well become the next issue.

Before **Photos 4.3** and **4.4** were taken I had done the same realignment with Jo that I did with Carol, bringing her legs up over the front of the saddle, bringing them down again, and putting my hands on her to find neutral spine and also to check her understanding of bearing down. But, as you see in **Photo 4.3**, she very soon reverted to her hollow back. **Photos 4.1–4.4** show Jo's attempts to home in on the shoulder/hip/heel vertical line, and although she never quite makes it, she comes much closer than many riders. Because her shoulders are too far back she would topple slightly back in **Photos 4.1** and **4.3**, but she would topple slightly forward in **Photo 4.2**, and she might need to bring her lower leg slightly further back to be dead right in **Photo 4.4**. Many hollow-backed riders would be much more disorganised than Jo in the hip-to-heel part of the alignment, with their stirrups too long and their feet out in front of them, but Jo has held this quite well from her previous lessons.

I then asked Jo to rise and sit a few times as she was standing still, and it took us a little while to get to the good balance point that she is demonstrating in **Photo 4.5**. Her initial attempts were as hollow as **Photo 4.2**, and as we discussed earlier, this is one of the major issues in rising trot. The others concern the stability of the lower leg, and the way the rider supports her body weight. In **Photo 4.6** I am exaggerating the most common version of rising-trot mechanism, and have pushed back on Jo's knee while pushing forward on her foot, thus illustrating the way in which many riders attempt to rise by pushing harder in the stirrup and straightening their knee. This makes their lower leg move forward on each rise, and as **Photo 4.6** shows, the rider cannot possibly get her pelvis over her foot when it is this far forward. So her centre of gravity remains behind her base of support, and she crashes back into the saddle again.

As Heather demonstrated in Chapter 2 (pages 38-39), in a biomechanically

Photo 4.5
Jo in balance at the top of the rise.

Photo 4.6 I exaggerate the tendency of many riders to push in the stirrup and straighten their knee as they rise. Using this mechanism, Jo could not remain in balance over her foot.

correct rise the knee acts as the centre point of the circle, and the thigh acts as a radius of that circle, and as it rotates over the knee, nothing from the knee down changes. The lower leg is not involved in either the rise or the sit; you could be amputated from the top of your boot and still do it well. The rider's pelvis moves forward and up on an arc of the circle, coming to the balance point that I call 'the top of the rise'. Every rise should reach this point, and should involve a thrust that matches the thrust of the horse's hind leg. This makes intuitive sense, but most riders are taught to make a much smaller rise, and the result is that either their horse does a tiny thrust to match them, or they get left behind as he races off. (There is more on this later.) In **Photo 4.5**, Jo is balancing at the top of the rise very well. However, once riders figure out how to rotate the thigh over the knee, their next problem is that they almost always hollow their back in the process, mirroring Jo in **Photo 4.2** rather than **Photo 4.5**.

The easiest way to understand and feel the difference is through the following exercise. (See **Fig. 4.3**) Kneel with your backside resting on your heels, and with some padding under your knees if necessary. Put the palm of one hand on your waistband at the front, and the back of the other hand on your waistband at the back. Your hands are there to check that your spine does not move, and that your upper body stays vertical. Now kneel up so that your pelvis is over your knees. Kneel up and down a few times, and notice how hard the quadriceps muscles at the front of your thighs are working. If you wish to, you can add to the torture and increase the training effect by pausing on the way up and/or the way down. In rising trot itself, your torso is inclined slightly forward in the sit and this reduces the strain on your thighs. However, I recommend that you do this kneeling exercise with your torso vertical, since this gives such a clear contrast to the way in which you are about to do it wrong. So try the more common version: lift your chin and stick it out, lift your chest and hollow your back. Let your chin and chest lead you into kneeling up, and notice how there is no more strain on your thighs! However, if you are prone to back pain, your back might well be complaining.

Rise again, using the hollow-backed mechanism, but this time stop just after

**Fig. 4.3**

(a) Begin by kneeling with your backside on your heels, and your hands on your front and back to help you maintain neutral spine.

(b) As you kneel up, be sure that you do not hollow your back or lean forward. If you repeat this a few times, your quads will soon let you know that they are working hard!

(c) In rising trot most people cheat by leaning forward, lifting their chin and chest whilst hollowing their back. There is now no strain on the quads. The rider using this mechanism will not be able to swing her pubic bone up over the pommel, so it does not actually 'rise'.

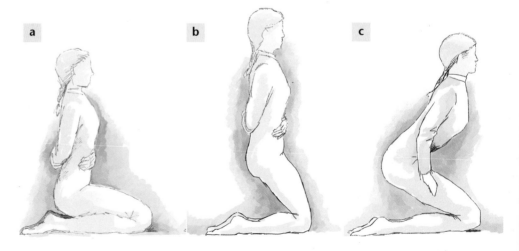

your backside leaves your heels. When riders rise like this, their pubic bone does not swing up over the pommel of the saddle – in fact it goes down and back instead of forward and up – so their rise can only go this far before they get stuck! But ninety per cent of riders do this stilted rise, pulling themselves up with the muscles of their chest and abdomen, and avoiding the work that their thighs have to do when they lever up the torso. If this remains box-shaped (i.e. if their front does not lengthen and their back does not hollow) their thighs have to work hard, and this is an idea that should have a familiar ring to it.

As we said in Chapter 2, the horse may prefer to pull himself along by lengthening the muscles of his stomach, chest and neck, and lifting his chin while hollowing his back. He too might prefer to avoid the more athletic movement that he could make if he kept his underside short, his topside long, and pushed himself along with his hind legs. The horrible feeling of the exercise where you imitated a hollow-backed horse **(Fig. 4.1)** might make you think that no living creature would choose to move like this; but if you have hollow-backed tendencies the chances are that you and your horse are a matching pair.

It is this correlation that I want the rider to understand, not just in her brain, but also in her body. A hollow-backed rider is usually found on a hollow-backed horse because they are both using their bodies in the same way, and if, as a rider, you *refuse to hollow* you can prevent the horse from being able to hollow under you. A rider like Heather does this well and makes it look so easy; but most riders begin to baulk when changing the way they do rising trot gives them their first introduction to core muscle strength. To *not* lengthen your front requires strength not only in the quads, but in muscles that lie deep inside the abdomen and pelvis. This is often the moment when reality hits home with a new pupil, and she becomes 'conscious of her incompetence'; riding is not as easy as she thought it was, her years of instruction have not even shown her how to do rising trot, and this requires a level of muscle power (within an apparent contortion) that she had not even conceived of. What is more, her plight is about to get worse as she discovers that even more muscle power is needed.

Let us suppose that the rider 'kneels' up and down well, and can maintain the balance point of **Photo 4.5**. When she does find this position, I then check the amount of weight in her stirrup, and there is almost always too much. I have been known to increase the rider's motivation by putting my fingers between the sole of her boot and the stirrup, while making it clear that I value my fingers and will scream if they hurt! When I then ask the rider to go to the top of the rise and balance there, she has to find another way to support her body weight; so she has to use her inside thighs. While her backside is in the saddle the whole of her thigh is in contact; at the top of the rise about two-thirds of it is in contact, and in each case that *entire length must be weight-bearing.* Sad to say, some people are not strong enough to support their body weight like this, while others panic about the thigh being against the saddle in a way that can feel like gripping. All I want the rider to do is to come as close as she can to the mechanics you saw in Heather; but the chances are that I have slain some sacred cows and turned her world upside down in the process.

Even if I have 'won the battle for hearts and minds', and my rider is prepared to work hard, to feel strange, and to renounce all the mistakes that she has worked so hard to learn, there is still going to be a battle with her muscles, and this will hinge on her breathing pattern. The hollow-backed rider is usually an upper-chest breather who lifts her ribs with each in-breath. This means that she hollows her back with each in-breath, and that all attempts not to hollow doom her to fight herself. She has to change her breathing technique, and this is no mean task – for you will not breathe one way twenty-three hours a day and then get on your horse and breathe differently in hour twenty-four. This means that you have to change how you breathe, period!

A number of ideas can help here, and in the previous chapter I suggested thinking of breathing down into a chemistry flask that lies within your pelvis, imagining that the air goes all the way down the long neck and into the round bowl. (See **Fig. 3.2**) Or imagine that you have gills like a fish, and put your hands against the back of your ribs with your thumbs pointing down and your little fingers along the line of the imaginary gills. Feel your back expand against your hands as you breathe in. As you breathe out, make the sound 'Psssht!', and feel how your back pushes against your hands even more strongly. This sound keeps you bearing down as you breathe out, and as your ribs deflate towards the end of the out-breath, prepare to keep bearing down as you breathe in, taking the air all the way down to the bottom of the flask. You can also think of your diaphragm, which is like the cap of a mushroom, forming a cross-membrane at the level of your hands. It is drawn *down* in each in-breath, making room for your lungs to inflate, but upper chest breathers tend to lift it up. Think of it like a parachute lying on the ground. If the wind gets underneath it, it billows up, but you must not let this happen. It has to be held down as you breathe in.

The effort it can take to learn to bear down and breathe at the same time is not to be underestimated, and the ability to do this underpins good riding skills. (You might like to look at *For the Good of the Rider*, where I wrote the stories of several people who really struggled with it, and told how they overcame the odds.) Lengthening your front and lifting your ribs has a devastating effect: do it now as you sit in your chair, and realise how it makes you suck your stomach in, and makes your breathing virtually stop. If you want to learn to ride really well you have no choice but to learn how to bear down continually while using abdominal breathing and keeping neutral spine. This is like throwing a six on a board game, which then enables you to start playing, and it has to become a life-skill that you practise off-horse.

So as Jo walked on I was able to give her a number of reminders that would help her to maintain this, and the following litany will contain some trigger words that are almost guaranteed to reach the brainscape of any hollow-backed rider. To begin at the top of the body: chin down, chest down, breathe down, keep your belly button back, bring your waistband back, round your back, feel slouched and/or short, tuck your backside under you. Keep your seat bones pointing down, keep thinking of your underneath from the back towards the front (as I suggested in the lesson with Carol). As you land in rising trot keep your pubic bone out in front of you – do not bury it back between your legs as you sit. As you rise, keep your pubic bone leading the way and do not let your belly button get ahead of your pubic bone. This makes your torso curve forward like a banana, but you want to keep it shaped like a box. Imagine my hand on your lower back pushing you up to the top of the rise, and think of opening the angle between your thigh and torso as you rise. The rider often has to thrust more than she ever imagined possible, and many people are extremely reluctant to thrust so much that they get to the balance point at the top of the rise.

**Photo 4.7** shows Jo in walk, holding the shape of both her own back and Erica's. Both of them have their chins down, and their stomachs short. It would be better if Jo were 'kneeling' more, and she could close her armpits a bit more at the back; but it is good to see her arms looking more a part of her, with a contact instead of a loopy rein. Erica's ears are not quite sideways, but her attention is much more internally directed than it is in **Photo 4.1**. Riders at this level often struggle to organise both their body and the horse. They have to keep his attention, keep enough impulsion, and keep the bit acting like the lid on the end of a tube of toothpaste that stops the toothpaste from leaking out.

There is another dimension to the problem that faces hollow-backed riders. When they bring their waistband back, as Jo has done well, their knee tends to come up; and when they then bring their knee down so that they 'kneel' more, their waistband then comes forward. It can seem impossible to keep the knee and the waistband apart, and this can become a game of ping-pong that has no end. The problem is short muscles, and the answer is to stretch the quadriceps muscles at the front of the thigh, and the psoas muscles which lie within the

Photo 4.7
As Erica begins to reach into the rein in walk, both she and Jo are no longer hollow-backed.

**Fig. 4.4**
The psoas muscle is the only muscle that attaches your spine to your legs. If it is short and tight, you will find yourself taking the hollow out of your back but discovering that your knee then comes up, or 'kneeling' well but discovering that your back then hollows.

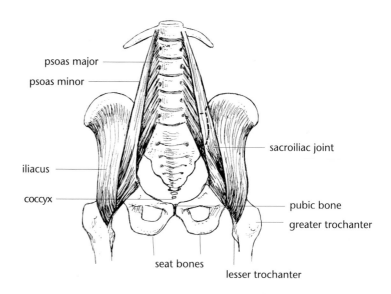

body cavity. (See **Fig. 4.4**) The safest and most effective stretches are done lying down, but since I know that you are less likely to do them that way, **Figs 4.5** and **4.6** show the best standing stretches. However, the disadvantage of the standing versions is that it is easy to cheat and avoid stretching the right muscles.

I had one more suggestion to help Jo keep the hollow out of her back *and* keep 'kneeling'. In **Photo 4.8** she is pushing her fingers into the crease between her torso and thigh to find the tendon that attaches the quadriceps muscle into the front of her pelvis. Put your own fingers there now, and then lift your knee just an inch or two. You should feel the tendon stick up like a taut piece of rope. (Actually there are two tendons, but you may have to poke yourself quite hard to feel them both.) Then put your other hand on your knee, as I have my hand

**Fig. 4.5**
(a) To stretch the quadriceps muscle at the front of the thigh, hold onto a support with one hand, and hold your foot in the other. Use a strap if you cannot reach. Keep your backside under you as you maintain the stretch for thirty seconds. Repeat four times. Take care that you do not hollow your back and cheat, as shown in (b).

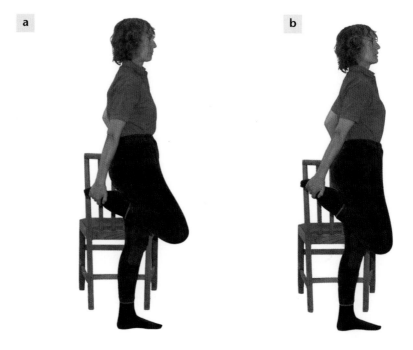

**Fig. 4.6**
To stretch psoas, begin by standing with your feet about three feet apart. Rotate one foot through 90°, and then turn your body to face in the same direction. Now lunge forward over that foot, keeping your hips level. Your back leg should ideally be straighter than mine is here. You may need to experiment (carefully) to find the precise position that gives you a stretch in the groin area of your back leg, where my fingertips are resting.

on Jo's knee, and without actually lifting your knee, push it up against that resistance. The tendons should again stick up, and if you look at the top of the quadriceps muscle, it changes shape becoming more triangular rather than flat. I also like to suggest that riders think of strong elastic cords which wrap around the tendons and pull them towards the horse's ears.

Lifting up the front tendons helps the hollow-backed rider to keep her pubic bone up, and it increases the tone and strength in the quads. The pull of those imaginary elastics helps the rider to 'kneel' out of the horse's 'man-trap', making the thigh a more effective lever. Then, the weight that acts at the knee counterbalances the weight of the torso that is stacked up at the other end of the lever arm. Without this leverage, the torso can act like a weight that

**Photo 4.8**
Pushing the knee up against a resistance, whilst feeling the 'front tendon' that inserts the quadriceps muscle into the front of the pelvis.

**Photo 4.9**
Finding the front tendon and the 'back corners' of the rider's backside, whilst sitting so that the front tendons are up and the back corners are down.

**Photo 4.10**
When the front tendons drop down the back corners of the backside come up and the rider hollows her back. Thinking 'back corners down, front tendons up' helps to stop this from happening.

squashes the horse's back down, creating or perpetuating his 'man-trap'. Simply by *not squashing it down* you help to draw it up, and this in turn puts more stuffing up the horse's neck. So I like to tell riders that 'If you can bulge your quads you can bulge the horse's neck.' Sometimes this simple idea works like a charm, for it is the laws of physics in action.

In **Photo 4.9** I have taken the idea a stage further, and have got hold of Jo's breeches, both where that front tendon lies and also on what I call the 'back corners' of her backside. If her torso were a box, these would be its back corners, and they need to stay down on the saddle. **Photo 4.10** shows what happens when the back corners come up and the front tendons go down, as happens when the rider's back hollows – and indeed, Jo's back has hollowed so much that you can now see a tree that had been obscured by her waistband! If she can keep those back corners down while those front tendons are up and pulled towards the horse's ears, she has much more ammunition to counteract her tendency to loose her 'kneel', her back, or both.

**Photo 4.11** shows Jo in rising trot looking much less hollow and 'kneeling' more effectively, and it also shows Erica producing the beginnings of a reach into the rein. Notice too how her tail is carried rather than being clamped to her hindquarters, as it was in **Photo 4.2.** She is still some way off tracking up, but if she were more active Jo would probably struggle to match her power. This concept might make more sense if you think of the rider/horse interaction as being rather like two people playing a co-operative game of catch with a tennis ball. Each one throws the ball with the same amount of impetus, and so that it bounces once in between them. But imagine that one of them suddenly throws the ball with more or less impetus, so that it bounces much higher, or 'dies' in the bounce. A speedy horse might throw the ball so that the rider cannot cope with the enormity of its bounce, while a lazy one might cause the ball to 'die'.

When riders do not thrust enough in the rise, and/or if they land heavily in the saddle, it is as if they throw the ball and make it 'die'. Many more riders do this than make it bounce too much, and any discrepancy between horse and rider gets them both into trouble. So the rider must gain control not only of the way in which both she and the horse throw the ball, but also of the *speed* of their throws.

The power of the thrust and the speed of the thrust determine the trot. Jo's tendency was to land slightly hollow and to get 'pinged' out of the saddle by Erica, who could then gain control of the trot, taking faster and shorter steps than Jo would have liked. In effect, Erica threw the ball back to Jo faster, and with more bounce. This then bounced Jo out of the saddle – so unwittingly, she threw it back faster as well. This gave them the potential to keep 'pinging' each other into a faster and faster trot! Whenever the rider lands with a hollow back she is vulnerable to this, and the answer is to bring those back corners down and to think of a *pause* in the saddle each time you land. Imagine Velcro between your backside and the saddle. In the opposite scenario where the rider crashes back into the saddle without controlling her descent, she has to make her thigh a more effective lever, keeping her knee in place and those front tendons up. To control how both of you 'bounce the ball' is a delicate business, but done well

**Photo 4.11**
Jo and Erica have both taken the hollow out of their backs, and instead they are doing a slight abdominal crunch. This has elongated Erica's top-line, giving her the beginnings of a reach into the rein.

it sets up a trot, and sets up a back, that you can then hope to sit on.

Jo did well in this session, and she will need many more like it to help her make the transition from being what I call 'a good up-down' to being a good rider. The first can do rising trot mechanism reasonably well; the second can use it to influence and shape the horse. This ability is as much about rights as about technique, for until you believe in yourself the horse will not believe you – so the rider who lacks experience may have to *act as if she knows how to do it*, and *act as if she has the right to do it*; and then the horse might take her seriously. It is a leap of faith; but without it, the horse will dismiss you as a novice. In truth, they read each of us like a book, and as we develop skill we learn to read – and influence – them with the equivalent sensitivity and power. Roll on that day, for Jo and the rest of us!

# CHAPTER 5

# Rounding the back | Millie

I HAVE TAUGHT MILLIE in two previous clinics, one and three years before this one. On each occasion I felt that she was one of the few people that I did not really get through to, and that the changes we made had not reached the 'critical mass' that convinced her of their importance. In each case I suspected that she felt more tortured than helped, and despite my attempts to sweeten the 'back to basics' pill that I was offering, its taste was too bitter at that time.

In the intervening time she has watched me teach on several clinics, and has seen the improvements in others. She has also retired from her business, which has given her much more time to devote to her riding, and she has begun working with a trainer who appreciates that she finds it particularly difficult to organise her body. So Millie's trainer has encouraged her to work with me. Although Millie has been very successful in business, she believes that she has learning difficulties, and it is certainly my experience that she does not find it easy to take in information, and that she is slow to process new ideas. She feels that she has been helped by doing exercises based on the work of Dr Paul Dennison (www.braingym.org), which utilise the movements of cross-crawl to integrate both brain hemispheres. These movements help to get them both 'switched on' at the same time, enabling you to both think and do simultaneously. Millie and I made an agreement at the beginning of the clinic that if she felt I was overloading her, or asking for verbal feedback that she could not give while riding, she was to grunt at me, and I would get the message! On several occasions, she did just this.

Millie's horse, Incognito, is a sixteen-year-old warmblood whom she has owned since he was seven. However, various injuries have caused to him to have three years off during this time. She is showing him at Third level (Medium level in the UK), and she began the clinic by saying that she wanted to be effective in half-halts. She rode in a double bridle because she was worried that he might become strong in this new environment, making it harder for her to learn. At home, she mostly rides in a snaffle. While this bridle and noseband

**Photo 5.1**
As Millie begins her lesson in walk, she is both rounding her back and leaning back.

would not be my choice of tack, I did not want to suggest a change that might undermine her confidence. Neither did I want to begin the clinic by putting us at odds.

Millie's default is the opposite of everything we have seen so far. **Photo 5.1**, taken in walk, shows her both rounding her back and leaning back. As she 'sits on her pockets', her seat bones point forward, and when she falls back down the 'man-trap' the front of her body gives way as if someone had punched her in the stomach. For her, this collapsed position is 'home'. As riders, we are all like a chain that gives way in its weakest link: Carol's weak link is the front angle between her thigh and torso, which so easily closes when the horse pushes back at her; Jo's weak link is the centre of her back, which so easily becomes hollow, and Millie's weak link is the centre of her *front*, which so readily collapses back. All of these fatal flaws characterise us as riders, determining how we place ourselves in the saddle even when the horse is not moving. Many teachers or trainers would just accept that this is how the person is, and would get on with teaching her the aids and the school movements. My major concern, however, is to help the rider become aware of her default, and then to evolve beyond it. I want to show her how much it hampers her horse, and how much more 'ridable' he becomes when she can maintain the correct balance point and ride in neutral spine.

Millie has low muscle tone, and because of this, she finds it difficult to support her own body weight. She rides *heavy*, and she needs to hold herself up instead of relying on the horse to do this for her. If her skin were a bag, it would be full of something rather leaden or stodgy, and this quality makes her too 'down'. The key issue for Millie is to firm up her muscles, finding higher isometric muscle tone. This will change their texture, bringing it closer to putty, and making her a firmer, lighter bundle. This in turn will give her far more

**Photo 5.2**
In rising trot Millie's knee has come up, making her thigh almost horizontal. In the sit phase her torso is vertical instead of inclined slightly forward, and this puts her behind the movement.

muscle control – but it is a snowball that is hard to get rolling. Muscle tone (and its role in stability) is *the* unacknowledged variable in riding, so it is not surprising that so many people find it elusive. Both mentally and physically, it is a difficult concept to grasp. This lack of tone underlies Millie's round back, and is her fatal flaw.

Somehow, Millie has to extract strength out of weakness, and this is particularly difficult because neither her brain nor her muscles know that isometric strength exists. It is an undiscovered, unexplored dimension of experience. She is like the blind man who must somehow discover blue, and I have found that this particular shade of blue is extremely difficult for the coach to explain. This is where my previous two clinics with her were limited in their success. Both Carol and Jo naturally have higher tone, and despite their obvious problems, this gives them an advantage. The accompanying disadvantage is that they have the tendency to be 'up' riders. So while Millie remains too 'down' if things go wrong, they vacate the saddle in moments of stress, either by tipping forward (Carol), or by hollowing (Jo). Only a few riders, like Heather, have 'up' and 'down' in perfect balance. This comes from sitting in neutral spine and using the whole length of her thigh to help her support her body weight.

The shape of the female spine and pelvis makes women naturally more hollow-backed than men, and more women hollow their back than round it. There may be cultural factors here too, and I have found that on the East coast of the USA a very high percentage of women are hollow-backed, while on the West coast an unusually high percentage are round-backed. Fewer women in the UK show the extremes I have seen in the USA. My observations of Americans are analogous with the way that those living in the West think that their East coast colleagues are uptight (and hollowing the back is an uptight posture); while those in the East have to concede that West coast dwellers are more laid back (and 'just hanging out' in that round-backed way!).

Millie is the exception to that rule, but she is an example of the way in which women with very low tone are the most likely to become round-backed. Her posture off horse is very good, and she blames her round back on her determination to keep holding up the heads of several horses who were extremely heavy in her hand! In men, tucking the backside under too much is the most common default, but in doing this they do not usually cave in the front of the body as much as women. As well as being built less hollow-backed, men have other reasons for not wanting to sit on their crotch – however, in my experience, they can sit in neutral spine without damaging themselves; they just need faith that they are working with a teacher who has their best interests at heart!

In **Photo 5.2** Millie is in the sit of rising trot and, although her back is less rounded, her shoulders are directly over her hips, as I would expect them to be while *sitting* but not while rising. This suggests that she is behind the correct balance point. Notice that her backside and shoulders are way behind her foot, and that her thigh bone is more horizontal than the ideal 45° angle. So instead of her weight being spread down through her thigh, it has become concentrated on her backside. Her leg position was much closer to right in **Photo 5.1**, where, even though her upper body has collapsed back, her quadriceps muscles can sustain the muscular work involved in 'kneeling'. In walk, she can almost muster enough strength to do the equivalent of limbo dancing, but in the other gaits her thighs are not strong enough to sustain this. Only very strong male riders can 'limbo dance' so effectively that their thighs can counterbalance the weight of a torso that is too far back.

**Photo 5.3** is taken in canter right, and again it shows Millie less round-backed, but with her backside a long way behind her foot. As I look at this photograph, it is very clear to me that again, her thigh is not weight bearing, and

**Photo 5.3**
In canter right, Millie's torso is close to vertical, but her knee is too up and her foot is too forward. This concentrates her weight on her backside instead of spreading it down her thigh. Incognito has reacted by hollowing and pushing back at her.

she has lost the look of 'kneeling' that she had in **Photo 5.1**. **Photo 5.4**, which is taken in sitting trot, shows Millie really leaning back and rounding her back. Here, more than in the other photographs, her hand has come back as her body has come back. I knew that she regarded my basic tactic of 'rising trot therapy' as torture, and wanted to see if she might be happier sitting. But her response to those few moments was to say 'Please don't make me do this!' Millie feels much more comfortable in canter and walk than she does in trot. In walk, she can keep her thigh reasonably functional, and in canter she can keep her torso reasonably functional, as shown in **Photos 5.1** and **5.3**. **Photo 5.4** suggests that trot is the gait where both her thigh and her torso give way. Since trot is the gait in which she topples back the most, it is also the gait in which she feels most uncomfortable and ineffective.

It is in canter (**Photo 5.3**) that Incognito has hollowed the most, reacting most strongly to the way that Millie collapses backwards with her weight in his 'man-trap'. He is pushing back slightly in **Photos 5.1** and **5.2**, while **Photo 5.4** shows him overbent. The bridle may well be a factor in this, and it is easy to imagine how Millie and her horses have pulled on each other, rather like the two people shown in **Fig. 5.1**. Many people might consider the carriage of **Photos 5.1, 5.2** and **5.4** to be good enough; however, **Photos 5.9** and **5.10** offer a contrast which shows how different Incognito looks when he does indeed lift his back and reach his neck out of his wither. With more stuffing up his neck he looks like a far more impressive horse, who would probably cost more to buy than the horse in the early photographs. This, I tell people, can make their clinic a good investment, and every horse – whatever his make, shape and breeding – develops the silhouette of an impressive dressage horse when he comes into the 'seeking reflexes'.

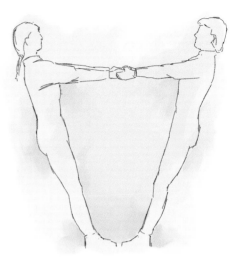

**Fig. 5.1** In Photo 5.4 *(below)* Millie and Incognito are interacting like two people who join hands and lean back against each other.

**Photo 5.4**
In sitting trot Millie is leaning a long way back as she rounds her back, and Incognito has reacted by overbending. You can see how much she clings onto his sides with her lower leg.

The concept of stuffing is a metaphorical way to talk about the tone in the horse's muscles, and if you think of a stallion prancing in front of a mare, you are witnessing the ultimate in high tone, where the horse looks like a brand new stuffed-toy horse. One of Heather's skills is the ability to put stuffing into a horse, and in top-level competition almost all of the horses will be well stuffed – partly by virtue of elite breeding, and partly by virtue of the way in which they are ridden. Only a well-stuffed rider can maintain this amount of muscle tone in the horse, and then stay 'with' the power she has generated. If you are less stuffed than your horse, you are likely to find him hard to control, and as he 'bursts out of his skin' he may well become intimidating (unless you can 'burst out of yours' and match him!). Millie is not a frightened rider, but increasing her tone will increase her confidence in her skills. If she can stay on the correct balance point she will become much more able to give her hand forward, and to stuff her horse so that he reaches into the rein. Last but not least, she will find the key to those elusive half-halts.

I watched Millie ride for a short time before I bought her to halt and re-aligned her body, helping her to find neutral spine. For her to maintain this, her thigh and lower leg had to change significantly. **Photos 5.5** and **5.6** show them before and after this change, which brings her knee and the front/inside of her thigh against the saddle, with her lower leg lying close to the horse's side but not against it, and her toe pointing forward. This puts her leg into the same position as Heather's in **Photo 2.3** (page 36). If you look again at **Photos 5.1 – 5 4**, you will see how firmly her lower leg is against the horse in each case. In fact, I have a very strong memory of the first time I taught Millie, and when I could not get her to maintain his change, I walked along beside her horse holding her lower leg slightly away from him. I was utterly amazed by how strongly the

**Photo 5.5**
From this angle you can clearly see how Millie takes her knee off the saddle and puts her calf against the horse.

**Photo 5.6**
The correction puts her thigh and knee against the saddle, with her heel much further away from the horse.

pattern of holding her leg against his side was 'wired in' for her, and also by the force she was using as she did this. It was incredibly hard for her to let her leg *hang* instead of *cling*.

Millie cannot change her leg position without changing her pelvis, and conversely, she cannot change her pelvis without changing her leg. While sitting on a chair, you can easily discover how this connection works, for when you round your back your thighs, knees, and toes roll outwards, while if you hollow your back they roll in, putting you into a knock-kneed and pigeon-toed position. Thus the riders who are most likely to grip with their knees are those who are hollow-backed, and this tendency is exaggerated if they are also nervous. Whenever the rider rolls onto the back of her backside and points her seat bones forward, her thighs, knees and feet will rotate out. Thus the rider's thigh comes away from the saddle, and the back of her calf comes against the horse, as we see here in **Photo 5.5**.

Many riders are taught to adopt this leg position, perhaps to ensure that they will not grip or pinch with their knees. But there are dangers in both extremes, and I think that skilled riders who place the thigh and calf really well have not discovered good ways to explain what they do so naturally. If you look at photographs of top-class riders, you will find that they all place the thigh as Heather does in **Photo 2.3**; it is against the saddle, but not gripping. The biomechanics of skilled riding have not changed over the centuries; good riders always have, and always will, use their body in essentially the same way. However, the ways in which we *describe* it have changed, as it becomes fashionable to emphasise first one element, then another. So as a child, I (like Jo) was taught to grip with my knees, and I think it was in the early 1970s that there was a sudden change in tune, with riders being told to 'relax their thigh and take their knee off the saddle'.

The following is a story which I made up, but I suspect that it has more than a grain of truth in it, and it explains the way in which *each school of thought has one half of the truth, expressed very poorly in language*. 'Grip with your knees', which was the old army teaching, described the use of the inner thigh muscles, but it implied that the knee must be more firmly on the saddle than the rest of the thigh. When this happens, the rider becomes like an old-fashioned clothes peg, and she 'pings' up and off the saddle in a backwards direction. This effect has given 'grip with your knees' its bad reputation. I like to think of the thighs being *snug* around the horse, and to do this they must be in an isometric contraction that narrows them in all the way from the corners of the pubic bone to the knee. They make a 'V' shape that widens out towards the knees, but is not so wide that the knees come off the saddle. However, the rider can dig her knees in so much that the arms of the 'V' become parallel. Remarkable as it sounds, the 'V' shape can even turn around, as if to make the knees narrower than the pubic bone and the rider's back. This defies logic (given the shape of a horse), but offers a good explanation of the 'clothes peg' effect. (See **Fig. 5.2** overleaf)

At the top of the rise the 'V' shape must not be so wide that there is nothing

**Fig. 5.2**
The rider's thigh bones ideally make a 'V' shape that has its point slightly behind her pelvis. But the bones can also be parallel, or they can feel as if they make a 'V' that has its point in front of the horse's chest.

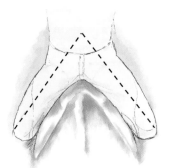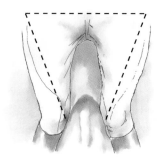

to stop the rider from crash-landing on her crotch. Neither must it be so narrow that the knee is the only weight-bearing point. The bottom two-thirds of the thigh support the rider's weight; but as we saw in the previous chapter, many riders do not have enough strength in these inner thigh muscles to support themselves effectively. The skilled riders who do will probably tell you that they are doing 'nothing'; but their 'nothing' is a very big 'something' for the person who has never trained these muscles. A 'Thighmaster' or a 'Pilates Magic Circle' are useful tools for developing this strength off horse, but even when using these it pays to remember the golden rule, which is that the knee must be no more firmly against the saddle than the top of the inside thigh. It is these muscles, right up by the corners of the pubic bone that the rider needs to train. This is where we can experience the discomfort of a lactic acid build-up, which is a sign that the muscles are working extremely hard. The demand on them is exaggerated when riding a remedial horse.

So in the early 1970s 'grip with your knees' went out of fashion, and I suspect that someone with considerable influence had a really good ride one day, and came out of it thinking 'But I didn't grip with my knees! I relaxed my thighs and took my knees off the saddle …'. So she told this to the most senior instructors, who told it to other instructors, who told it to the most junior instructors, and so it became the new norm. The sad thing is that she had never even heard of isometric muscle use, and just assumed that she had relaxed. If she had told us instead to think of *pushing the knee out against a resistance*, her discovery would have had a very different influence on the next generation of riders.

I am now implying that the knee and thigh are concurrently narrowing in, as if against a resistance, *and* pushing out, as if against a resistance. This strange result is what happens when the inner and outer thigh muscles are both used isometrically. So the inner thigh muscles bring the thigh into a snug 'V' shape around the horse's ribcage (drawing inwards to make contact with it), while the outer thigh muscles attempt to draw the ribcage out, into the 'seeking reflexes'. I often suggest that riders imagine they have suction cups on their inside thighs, suctioning them onto the horse's ribcage as they think of drawing it outwards. The paradox arises because *you cannot do suction on anything if you have not first made contact with it*; and if in the process you lose that contact, you have to narrow the thighs in, re-find the contact, and start all over again.

The lessons described later in this book show riders who are more established in this work, and there I place more emphasis on the role of the outer thigh. For them, good use of the inner thigh is already a given, and since their horses are also more established, my teaching can move into a deeper layer of the onion. But in the early stages of my work with a pupil, there is much more emphasis on the inner thigh. This has to right the wrong of their previous muscle use. Also, they (like the riders in the army) are usually riding less organised, and perhaps even remedial, horses, while the skilled riders who determine our dogma are more likely to be riding talented (or at least established) horses with whom one can emphasise the next stage. What is true on one layer of the onion can be highly misleading on another.

This change in the use of the thigh muscles leads to changes in how the rider uses her lower leg to give an aid. Millie tended to keep her calf in a continuous and strong contact with the horse's side, and I suspect that it became even stronger within a leg aid. I wanted her to keep her calf close to his side, and then to slap him with it in each leg aid. A slap can be more or less strong, but it always remains a quick in-and-out, as if you *bounce* the calf off the horse's side. Once you attempt to make the aid stronger by keeping the calf against his side for longer, you are no longer making a slap. You will also inevitably experience repercussions that involve the thigh muscles, and perhaps even the backside and torso. Only the slap keeps the lower leg independent of the rest of the body, which remains on the balance point as if nothing had happened.

It is the attempt to bring strength into the leg aid that gets the rider into all sorts of trouble as she lifts her heel, turns her toe out, and makes a prolonged squeeze. The rider's aim is to make a small, quick, effective movement. So in the following exercise pretend that your arms are your legs, and that your thighs are your horse's sides. Make a big, loose swing with your arms, and they will hit your thighs with very little 'clout'. Then make a smaller, more dynamic, swing that hits your thighs harder, and make sure that you only move your lower arm. Many riders find the equivalent of this difficult to do with the lower leg. It takes practice, and significant muscle tone in the calf, for a leg that hangs like limp lettuce cannot make that quicker, more dynamic movement.

For Millie, the new way of using her lower leg is a big demand, for she will so easily use the (considerable) strength in her calves in the wrong way, and hold them against the horse's sides for too long. Then, her thighs open out, and she rolls back onto the back of her backside, exposing the weakness in the muscles of her front. This change puts her behind the correct balance point, and she has to make a massive correction to reorganise herself. Every leg aid then comes at a price, which she can only avoid if she can hold her thigh and torso in place as she gives the aid. To help her I suggested that she thought of her inside thigh draping down over the stirrup bar and forming part of her sitting surface, and also that she thought of *spiralling* her thighs down and in and onto the horse. This helped her to exaggerate the inward rotation that brings her closer to a knock-kneed, pigeon-toed stance. One of the thigh muscles (sartorius) does

**Photo 5.7**
In walk, Millie is now showing a shoulder/hip/heel vertical line, although her reins are rather long, and her lower leg is still against her horse's side.

indeed make a spiral, running from the top outside of the thigh to the inside of the knee, and Millie must keep this muscle engaged as she uses her lower leg.

Millie's tendency to roll onto the back of her backside and to roll her thighs outwards is so strong that I do not think she will ever over-correct to make the mistake of gripping with her knees. But her horse needs her to create a 'V' shape that can contain and channel him, and it can help to think of this like putting him in an 'A' frame. Millie is not only too wide at her knees, she is also so wide in her back that, in effect, she is floating off the sides of the horse. The biggest success of our previous clinics was that she had begun to understand and change this; but more change was needed.

When the rider needs to become narrower across the back of her pelvis, I often suggest that she thinks of a corset with laces that would draw the two sides of her backside in towards each other. I used to call this 'the pinch', but now

**Photo 5.8**
In rising trot Millie has her torso inclined just slightly forward, putting her into a much better balance, although her knee is still a little too up.

refer to it as 'lacing up across the back'. Or she can think of the two sides being drawn together by one of those butterfly hair clips, with teeth, that people use to hold up their hair. In your quest to make the perfect 'A' frame it usually helps to think of being narrow across your back, narrow between your seat bones (there will be much more on this later), narrow at the top inside thigh, and narrow all the way down to the knees, creating an even pressure along that snug inner thigh. Once your back has narrowed, think of pushing the back of you towards the front of you as if you had no thickness. Think of a man wearing a sandwich board, and imagine the back board pushed up towards the front board, particularly at the level of the pelvis. Thinking of the forward push of your bear down beginning in your back can double its power. These ideas had helped Millie on our previous clinics, and she had kept working with them; but she needed to bring them to mind and strengthen their effects.

**Photo 5.7** shows Millie in walk, in exactly the same phase of the stride as **Photo 5.1**. The change in her torso following the realignment is obvious, and notice how her kneecap aims towards the point of the horse's shoulder instead of towards the base of his neck. Her toe is still pointing out with the back of her calf against the horse, but the other photos suggest that, overall, this effect is lessening. Her horse is reaching into the rein more convincingly, perhaps because his ears are sideways rather than pricked, and perhaps because her body weight is much less down his 'man-trap'. **Photo 5.8,** taken in rising trot, shows Millie with a slight incline forward in her upper body, and much closer to being in balance over her foot. Her horse is far from tracking up, but at the moment she would probably struggle to match that extra power (remember that game of catch), and she will do better to add this in increments as she gains the strength that makes her less vulnerable to the collapse that topples her backwards.

Her 'pièce de resistance' was the canter in **Photos 5.9** and **5.10**, where Incognito is so much more stuffed and reaching into the rein. **Photo 5.10** shows

Photo 5.9
Comparing this canter with Photo 5.3 shows just how much Millie and Incognito have both changed. Now that she supports her own body weight he can come up through his back and reach into the rein.

**Photo 5.10**
Millie still needs to bring her lower leg more back under her, but her torso is on the correct balance point. Her horse looks much more stuffed than he did in the early photos, although he is slightly overbent.

almost the exact same moment in the stride as **Photo 5.3**, albeit on the other rein. Millie has radically changed her way of sitting and she is reaping great rewards for this. See how her weight is taken so much more in her thigh. You can see that the tone of the muscles in her backside and thigh has changed – they really do look less 'soggy'. She is still not quite in balance over her foot, and to make herself more like Heather she has to bear down more, 'kneel' more, rotate the thigh in more, and become much stronger in that posture. You might criticise her horse for being slightly overbent, but I have met many people who would give their eye teeth to change their horse this much! (The question is, would they also give their back, stomach and thigh muscles?)

Over the course of the three days we built on this change, and it was in canter that Millie first began to ride some effective half-halts. They led to a radical change in her thinking, for like most riders, she had imagined that bringing her horse's weight back required her to come more back. But in reality, she was too far back already. On several occasions what was intended as a position correction actually became a half-halt, and Millie found what she began to call 'the sweet spot'. This caused Incognito to pause for a moment under her, slowing the tempo and sitting down. 'Oh!' was her response to the first of these, and the 'Ooohhs!' grew in intensity as she gained a deeper appreciation of the way that she was actually doing the *opposite* of what she had expected. Instead of bringing the horse back to her (and probably collapsing backwards herself in the process), she had attempted to realign herself by strengthening her 'kneel' and the push from her back. In the process of this she had caught up with the horse.

The moment her centre of gravity came *over* his instead of behind it, he instantly responded, and this realisation turned her previous thinking on its head.

It will take Millie quite some time to be able to ride half-halts in each gait and on each rein, and to ride them to order. But at least now she knows what they are, and knows that she has to look for them in a different way and a different place. It is so imperative, and so difficult, for the low-tone rider to discover the hidden dimension of isometric muscle tone, and its role in holding the body on (or, in the case of these half-halts, returning it to) the correct balance point.

Much to the delight of Millie and myself, the blind man has now discovered blue.

# CHAPTER 6

# Leaning back | Diane

Diane is an accomplished rider who works in partnership with a Dutch colleague importing horses into America. It is a precarious way to earn a living, and she is a nomad, renting stables in other people's barns and living between New Jersey in summer and Florida in winter. But she loves the way that it gives her the opportunity to ride a succession of very nice horses – although the downside is that she has to stop herself from becoming too fond of them! Royal Dancer is a seven-year-old Dutch gelding who she had been riding for four months, and he was sold to a professional rider soon after the clinic.

I had taught Diane twice about three months before this clinic, again on Dancer, so this was her third lesson. She wants nothing more than to ride as well as she can, and she is much more willing than many professionals to admit to the limitations of the biomechanical skills she already possesses. In those first two lessons she proved a very good pupil, and she quickly realised how changing her body could change the horse profoundly, giving her more tools to improve him than the school movements alone. In fact, I felt very flattered when a few months after these photographs were taken, she had a lesson with me on the day that she had an evening flight to Germany. She was about to spend three months training with one of the dressage world's great names. She knew that my work would help her to make better use of the training input she would receive there, where the issues with her body were unlikely to be addressed – just as they had not been addressed in the past.

**Photo 6.1** shows Diane in canter, looking very polished, and much more like 'a dressage rider' than other riders who have illustrated the defaults. Some might think that she looks just as effective as Heather, but in my view she shares with many dressage riders (including Heather in our first lesson) the fourth default. This gives us a full set, with their pelvic positions shown in **Fig. 6.1** – (a) = Heather, (b) = Carol and Jo, and (c) = Millie and Diane). Diane opens the front angle too much and this tips her back; but it does so without her lumbar spine

**Photo 6.1**
Diane looks very polished, but she is leaning back, growing too tall, and stretching her leg down too much. This allows Dancer to dive down onto his forehand, lifting his croup even more as the leading foreleg becomes the only weight-bearing leg in canter.

**Fig. 6.1** The seat bones.

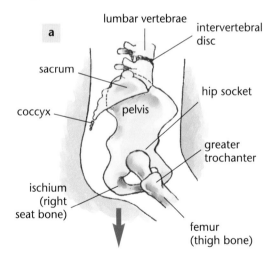

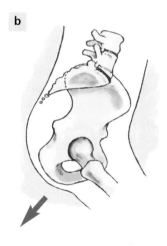

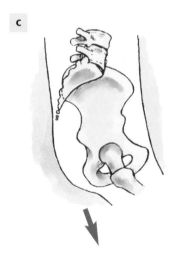

(a) Heather sits in neutral spine, with her seat bones pointing straight down. Less than three per cent of riders sit like this, but it is the foundation of the most effective and horse-friendly sitting.

(b) Both Carol and Jo sit with their seat bones pointing back. Carol tips forward as she closes the front angle, and Jo hollows her back. Some riders combine these two defaults.

(c) Both Millie and Diane sit with their seat bones pointing forward. Millie rounds her back and slouches back, and Diane leans back as she opens the angle between the thigh and torso. Leaning back whilst hollowing the back could cause the seat bones to point either forward or back, depending on which pattern dominates.

**Photo 6.2**
In rising trot early on in the session, Diane is not quite in balance over her foot. She has made the movement of the rise by pushing in her stirrup and straightening her knee. With these biomechanics, it is impossible for her to counteract Dancer's tendency to overbend.

giving way. When Millie tips back, it is as if she has a hinge in her middle, which collapses her front, and shortens it relative to her back. The same hinge puts Jo's torso into the reverse position, with a long front and a short back, and one of the fundamental skills of riding lies in keeping the torso box-shaped and stopping the lumbar spine from acting as a hinge. Like Millie, Diane's tip backwards tucks her backside under her too much and points her seat bones forward. But like Carol, her issue is more about the hinge of the hip joint than a hinge in the lumbar spine.

When Diane leans back she stretches up too tall, and stretches her leg down too long. When I first taught her she also hinged at her waist, lengthening her front more than her back, so that she combined the defaults of leaning back and hollowing the back. As I said in the Chapter on Jo, I call this a 'sophisticated hollow back'. (I now wish I had asked Diane to return to her old pattern and ex-aggerate the lifting of her ribs, making this clearer to your eye! However, if you compare **Photo 6.1** with **Photos 6.9** and **6.10** you can see how much less 'tall' she became as the lesson progressed.) As you diagnose yourself, you also need to discover how you too might combine two defaults. Some riders combine Carol's and Jo's defaults by leaning forward while hollowing the back; but leaning *back* while hollowing the back is a more complex pattern, for the rela-tive amount of each component will determine whether your seat bones end up pointing forward (from leaning back) or back (from hollowing your back).

Riders like Diane – and also hollow-backed riders like Jo – make me bemoan the fact that what everyone knows about dressage is that you must grow tall and stretch your legs down. Later I will explain how these statements have validity once you are deep within the layers of the onion. But as Xs that have been pre-sented as As, they are inevitably misleading. The vast majority of riders hear the words and interpret them like Jo or Diane, and this unseen, unacknowledged distortion between the wordscape and the brainscape limits the skill of many riders, spanning the entire spectrum from 'happy hackers' to professionals. What saddens me the most is that so many of them have worked extremely hard to do what they were told.

**Photo 6.2** shows Diane in rising trot, nearing the top of the rise. To my eye, her ribcage looks more compact than it does in **Photo 6.1**, but she is still stretching down too much with her leg. There is too much weight in her stirrup, and this has compromised the action of her knee, hip and ankle joints. So in the rise she pushes in the stirrup and straightens her knee (as I demonstrated with Jo in **Photo 4.6**). Instead, she needs to keep her foot resting more lightly in the stirrup, and to rotate her thigh over her knee on that arc of a circle. Some people find that it works well to think of 'kneeling' up and down as if resting on a kneeler in church. When corrected, her left leg will look like her right leg does in **Photo 6.3**. This was taken as she was warming down at the end of the session. The angles of her hip and knee joints look more distinct, which shows how well her joints are working, and how lightly her foot rests in the stirrup.

Diane clearly finds it easy to open the front angle between her thigh and torso, and as the inverse of Carol who struggled so much with this, the muscles of the front of her torso are probably longer than those of her back. At the top of the rise in **Photo 6.3**, she is marginally behind the ideal knee-to-hip-to-shoulder vertical line, but I suspect that she would have overshot it more in the rise of **Photo 6.2**. Dancer is noticeably less downhill in **Photo 6.3** than **Photo 6.2**, although the angle under his gullet could still be a little more open, giving him more reach into the rein as he warms down. **Photo 6.4**, taken in sitting trot in the early part of the lesson, shows Diane looking very polished, but actually at her most disorganised: she is clearly leaning back, with her shoulders behind her backside, which is behind her foot, with her heel far too down and forward. If we took her horse out from under her by magic she would land on her back-

Photo 6.3
As she warms down at the end of the session, Diane shows a more correct rising trot mechanism, and she has reached the correct balance point at the top of the rise. She has less weight in her foot than she had in photo 6.2 and her joints are working more correctly. Dancer is still very slightly overbent.

**Photo 6.4**
In sitting trot, Diane is leaning slightly back with her backside tucked too far under her. Her heel is way too down and forward.

side and not on her feet.

So why am I so against this? If you look at Dancer in **Photos 6.1, 6.2** and **6.4** he is very overbent in all of them, and he has a rather downhill look. As they were all taken early on in the lesson this is not surprising; but the problem is that Diane cannot easily change this carriage. Being able to *choose* to lower a horse's neck and then *choose* to raise it is very different to not having that choice. In actual fact, Diane's alignment is contributing to the problem, and the masters of collection – of whom there are a few in every generation of riders – will rarely if ever be seen behind the vertical.

Let me explain the biomechanics of this. Imagine a rider going across the diagonal in medium or extended trot. Many riders lean back, bringing their centre of gravity back behind the horse's. To understand the dynamic this invokes, think of standing on a rug on a polished floor. When somebody pulls the rug out forwards from under your feet, you topple back, and the more you do this, the more the rug slides out from under you. You might have experienced the same effect on a skiing holiday, when your insides quake at the thought of going down the mountain. Instinctively you lean back, which sends you down the mountain faster than you would have gone if you had been brave enough to stay in balance over your skis! So if you lean back on your horse he too scoots out from under you, and in effect, you become like a waterskier who is towed along by the equine equivalent of a motorboat.

Should you be foolish enough to lean back more as the horse accelerates away from you, your body is – by the laws of physics – saying 'Go, go!' Even if you are pulling on the reins for all you are worth, and thinking that you are saying

'Whoa, whoa!', you are kidding yourself. (See **Fig. 6.2**) This mistaken impression is both instinctive, and accepted within our culture. Issue number one is that your pull may well make the horse claustrophobic, encouraging him to pull even harder against you; but even if this is not the case, issue number two is that your body position encourages the rug/horse/skis/motorboat to keep on accelerating away from you. In other contexts, most of us learn quickly that those who trifle with the laws of physics are doomed to lose the contest; but as riders we seem particularly slow to get the message!

When riders utilise the waterski/motorboat effect in an extension, they deliberately bring their centre of gravity back behind the horse's, and he accelerates out from under them, elongating his frame and his stride. But as he 'motorboats' he also flattens, with more weight than necessary on his forehand, which is why some riders – including Heather – choose to avoid leaning back. But the acid test comes at the end of the diagonal, when the rider has to collect the horse. What does she need to do then? Many riders again lean back in the mistaken belief that they are weighting the quarters. But if you do this to get an extension, it cannot be the best way to get collection! In fact, by the waterski/motorboat principle, the more you lean back, the more the horse goes out from underneath you, leaning on your hand and flattening. You might be tempted to curse him for his evasive nature and his lack of willingness to 'sit down'; but in reality, you played a major part in creating the pattern.

This is what Millie discovered when she stumbled, almost by accident, on the 'sweet spot'. She had thought that leaning back would get her the collecting effect of a half-halt; but she found it instead through the position correction that bought her torso forward and into neutral spine. Neither Incognito nor Dancer are archetypal motorboat horses who react to any waterski by whizzing

Fig. 6.2
This rider might think she is saying 'Whoa, whoa!', but by the laws of physics, she is actually saying 'Go, go!'. As she adopts 'waterski' position so the horse tows her along like a motorboat.

out from under the rider; and neither are they flighty enough to initiate those moments by 'pulling the rug out' themselves. Of all the horses in this book, Otto, Arabella and Erica have the greatest 'motorboat' tendencies, and with a less skilled rider Otto and Arabella might well have spent their lives whizzing their way around training level tests! They both needed an exceptional rider who could stay on the balance point when they accelerated, and slow down that game of 'catch'. Very few riders could have contained and channelled their inexhaustible energy, keeping up with them and matching their power in each stride. Only this has allowed them both to reach their potential.

Millie and Incognito have quietly maintained a more subtle waterski/motorboat interaction, where he pulls on her a little and she pulls on him a little, and collection eludes them (remember the drawing of the two people pulling against each other in the last chapter – page 87). Dancer has a rather different style, and instead of hollowing as he leans into the rein contact, he overbends, sometimes becoming heavy in the hand, and sometimes becoming too light. Like your tennis partner who plays to your weak backhand, your horse will have his most instinctive way to capitalise on your weakness (and unless you are extremely precise, he will learn a few more along the way!). The first step in countering each of these evasions is for the rider to advance her centre of gravity and bring it over the horse's. This is like bringing yourself up onto the crest of a wave. The rider who leans back to create extension deliberately brings herself *behind* the crest of the wave, and the wave rolls on ahead of her. Only when she comes up onto the crest of the wave can she draw the horse's wither up under her instead of sending it out ahead of her.

Diane had begun to grapple with these ideas in our last clinic, both in her riding and in the workshops, where we often use exercises to bring the theory to life. She had begun to question her understanding of riding, and she had made significant changes to her biomechanics. She had maintained some of these more than others, so after a short time I stopped her, and I began our work by taking her stirrups up one hole, which placed her thigh bone at that 45° angle. She was not sure if she had altered their length since our first clinic, when I had taken them up two holes. (Heather's stirrups, remember, went up three holes in her first lesson!) In our realignment, I brought her into a shoulder/hip/heel vertical line, and emphasised the need to keep her foot back under her and light in the stirrup. I wanted her to realise that to correct the position she showed in **Photo 6.4**, she literally had to bring her heel *back and up* (remember **Fig. 2.1**, page 33). This shocks many riders, and if you lack tone in your lower leg, it can be a difficult change to make. Bizarre as it sounds, it can be helpful to think of holding a wedge-shaped piece of Edam or Gouda cheese behind your knee, being sure that you do not let it go.

I also used the exercises shown in **Photos 6.5** and **6.6** to help Diane stabilise her torso. In **Photo 6.5** I am asking her to resist my push – replicating the partner exercise done on a gym ball on page 61. Realise too that if the horse accelerates out from under you, this is similar to someone attempting to push the

gym ball forwards out from under you, and the challenge in both cases is to stay vertical instead of toppling back. Diane needs to feel how her abdominal muscles must work to maintain the vertical position of neutral spine, which is not her 'home'. But there is more to this than her abdominals, and in **Photo 6.6** my hands are on a muscle called serratus anterior, which begins under the shoulder blade and comes around the sides of the ribs like a set of fingers. I am asking Diane to pull away from me as I pull back on her, and then to reproduce that feeling as she rides.

This is an advanced version of a similar exercise that I often use in workshops. Begin by reaching one arm across your front, and grab yourself just below the back of your armpit. You will find yourself putting your thumb and fingers around a muscle called the latissimus dorsi. If you then pull down your shoulder and pull down your elbow, the muscle should become more obvious as it bulks out into an isometric contraction. The 'lats' is a triangular sheet of muscle, whose edges run along each side of your spine, across your back at armpit level, and down your side to your pelvis. If your 'lats' are well developed, this bulking out of their edges will continue right down to your pelvis, but most people run out of muscle power at the level of their chest. (See **Fig. 6.3** overleaf)

**Photo 6.5**
Diane is resisting my backward push on her upper chest. This makes her activate the muscles that will stop her from leaning back.

**Photo 6.6**
Diane is pulling her torso forward against my backward pull on the muscle serratus anterior.

**Fig. 6.3**
These two drawings show the latissimus dorsi and the serratus anterior, and the way that you can reach across your chest and grab the edge of the 'lats'.

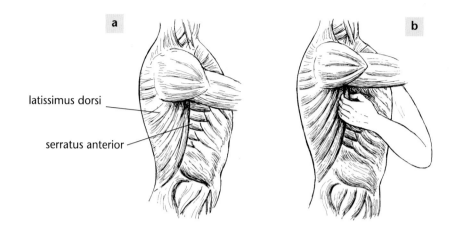

latissimus dorsi

serratus anterior

Now stand in an 'on-horse' position, with one foot slightly forward, and ask a friend to stand behind you, holding the muscle just below each armpit. Pull down your shoulders, pull down your elbows, and attempt to pull away from her – but be sure to stay vertical as you do so. Good riders use this forward force to help them stay 'with' the horse, and more skilled riders create even more forward force by doing the same with the serratus anterior. If you know your friend well enough to have her place her fingertips as I have done in **Photo 6.6,** you can reproduce that exercise too. You can also try pulling away from someone who has hold of your 'love handles'! The rider who exerts these forces does not lean forward, but she adds much more power to the forward force of bearing down. This now involves her abdominal muscles, much of her back, and her sides.

I wanted Diane to think of pulling away from these imaginary people as she rode, preferably using all of these muscles. To realise what this does for you, imagine walking on your feet on a conveyor belt. On the conveyor belt, your leg advances and your foot contacts the belt, which then draws your foot back underneath you as your torso passes over it. Now imagine that your legs have been amputated, and that you are walking on your seat bones. Each one steps forward, and then, as it is moved back by the belt, your torso advances over it. This is the way that a duck paddles itself forwards, and the way that your seat bones must move as you pull away from the imaginary people. Your seat bones move over your flesh, but neither your flesh nor your breeches move on the saddle, so an observer would not see any wiggling or jiggling of your backside. You remain 'plugged in', which means that you are *still relative to the horse,* with only the movement in your seat bones that his 'conveyor belt' gives you.

If instead you thought of pushing each seat bone forward – as most riders do – you would move your backside much more, jiggling or shoving it around. You think that you are generating forward motion, but ironically you have become like a duck who is paddling *backwards*. This would tend to bring your torso back behind your seat bones, and pulling away from the imaginary people no longer makes sense. But the idea of 'the driving seat' (or Müseler's famous image of 'pushing a swing') *would* make sense, and might indeed make your horse go

**Fig. 6.4**
Pulling away from someone who has grabbed hold of your 'lats' gives you a more effective way to 'keep up with the horse' in each stride.

forwards – just like a motorboat! When all else fails this may well be your best option, but when you look at Diane in **Photo 6.4**, its downside becomes obvious, for all of the force vectors in her body are *aiming directly towards the horse's front feet*. So if you are having dreams of collection, it pays to redirect those forces towards his *hind feet*. Think of walking on a conveyor belt and pulling away from the imaginary people; for as we know in other contexts, you will always suffer if you fight the laws of physics!

In Diane's lesson I also described the rider/horse interaction by comparing the rider's torso to a carousel pole, which connects right down through the horse. Whenever a motorboat type of horse accelerates, he hollows his back and lengthens his underneath, so his stomach is pulled forward towards his chest, and his chest is pulled forward towards his neck. This lengthens the underside of his torso and neck in much the same way that a hollow-backed rider lengthens her front. As the horse draws the bottom of the carousel pole forward, the rider, as the top of the carousel pole, then topples back. Conversely, when the top of the pole comes back, the bottom of the pole goes forwards, causing the horse to elongate these muscles. Usually this will put the horse against the hand as he hollows. We see this in Arthur and Erica, but (as I shall explain later) it may cause the horse to overbend like Dancer, or to have the choice of either response – as we saw with Incognito.

The rider who leans back usually has no idea that she has influenced the horse all the way down to his stomach muscles. But a highly skilled rider can knowingly influence the horse here too – for good rather than ill. If she *refuses* to let the top of the carousel pole topple back, the bottom of it cannot be pulled forward, and the horse cannot elongate his underneath. This forces him to remain in a carriage where his back is raised and he is light in the hand. It takes great core muscle strength for the rider to maintain neutral spine in the face of this onslaught – and I hope this argument helps to convince you that neutral spine is more than just a pretty way to sit. If you know how to look, you can see these effects in Heather's body, and her refusal to lean back on Otto and Arabella takes the kind of bear down that develops over years, involving the diaphragm and the deepest layer of muscles. Almost all riders begin the journey towards this kind of core strength from a starting point where they lengthen their front in each rise (as Diane did at the start of her first clinic, and as we discussed in the lesson with Jo). So perhaps it is clearer now how anything short of an *absolute refusal to do this* offers the horse an invitation to lengthen his abdomen as well.

As we look at Diane and her horse, we are now moving on a stage from the issues facing the riders who illustrated the other defaults. They were dealing with the first challenge, which is to learn how to get the horse's back up. Then, depending on your horse's evasive pattern, it is only a matter of time before you have to learn how to get the horse's *front* up. To do this Diane had to reposition the carousel pole, pull away from the imaginary people, and rearrange the force vectors acting in her body. Then, she could potentially change that waterski/motorboat interaction, and stop her horse from burying his forehand.

The ideas outlined above really help people (as I hope they have helped you) to rethink their understanding of the rider/horse interaction. They give a good overview, but Diane now needed more specific help to stabilise her torso in the face of her horse's desire to maintain the *status quo*. So I offered her a series of more specific images that I have found helpful over the years with horses who overbend.

The first builds on the idea of the carousel pole, and the horse who drags the bottom of the carousel pole forward also drags its middle forward and drags the rider's seat bones forward with it. By leaning back, Diane has tilted the way that her underneath contacts the saddle, and she is pointing her seat bones forward

Fig. 6.5
When the horse is ridden in a 'deep and round' carriage, or when he overbends as an evasion, his back can come up so much that the rider's underneath barely contacts it, as shown in (b). Think of it like a tangent barely touching an arc of a circle. The rider's underneath must make a longer, flatter surface that remains in contact with a longer flatter surface on the horse, as shown in (a). This can stop him curling away from under her pubic bone.

Photo 6.7
Diane is now much closer to right, with her heel more back under her, and her torso just a fraction behind vertical. Dancer is now in a much more uphill carriage, although he is not tracking up.

while lifting her pubic bone. In doing this she has, in effect, given Dancer permission to advance the bottom of the carousel pole as he curls his forehand down and away from her (disappeared) pubic bone. Like the rider in **Fig. 6.5(a)**, Diane has to keep her underneath flat on the saddle, partly by pulling away from the imaginary people, by 'duck paddling', and by thinking of the shape she wants to make in both her underneath and in his back and neck.

Having the horse's neck up rather than down changes the shape of his back, and gives the rider a longer, flatter surface to sit on. When the neck curls down only a small part of the back lifts, shaping it like an arc of a circle. When you want a hollow-backed horse to reach down, the way that you 'kneel' out of his 'man-trap' encourages him to make this shape, so it is the shape that riders first learn to create and feel. It is also the shape most riders make at the beginning and end of a session as they warm the horse up and down. But it is not the shape of collection.

If Diane tucks her backside under her and reduces the length of her sitting surface, her underneath becomes like a tangent that barely contacts that arc, and she becomes powerless to change its shape, as in **Fig. 6.5(b)**. In **Photo 6.1** very little of her underneath is contacting the saddle, and the challenge is to make it into a longer, flatter surface that remains in contact with his longer, flatter back. Unlike most riders, Diane has a tiny backside, but by lifting her pubic bone she had made it look even smaller than it actually is! You see this longer, flatter sitting surface in all of the photographs of Heather, as well as in **Fig. 6.5(a)**. But in **Photo 6.7** Diane is much closer to right, and she has made a fabulous difference to Dancer, who is now in a more uphill carriage. However,

**Photo 6.8**
I am demonstrating the idea of holding a tea tray between my thighs that must not be allowed to tip down, just as the horse's neck must not be allowed to tip down.

she needs to change the shape of her backside even more, or she will still be vulnerable to his pet evasion. Her pubic bone is still a little too lifted, her backside is still a little too under her, and she is a fraction behind the ideal of that pubic bone/belly button/sternum/collar bone straight vertical line. Dancer is still a fraction overbent, and I would like to see his hind leg looking as though he will track up. Diane has also made a very good correction to her lower leg, and if she now went into rising trot, her leg would (hopefully) make the shape shown in **Photo 6.3** not **Photo 6.2**.

The muscles in the lower part of the horse's crest, and also the muscles under the saddle, do a huge amount of work as they counterbalance the weight of his head. To help you empathise with this, hold your arm horizontally out ahead of you while holding a one litre bottle of spring water. You will soon realise that the muscles along the top of your upper arm are working very hard! Both your arm muscles and the horse's neck muscles tire quickly – hence the horse is likely to take the easy way out, either by letting you hold his head up, or by lowering it closer to the ground.

I wanted Diane to understand how her body position can encourage Dancer to counterbalance the weight of his head as he holds it up more, and as I explained my idea to her I adopted the position you see in **Photo 6.8**. My lower arms are horizontal, with my elbows between my thighs. Imagine my lower arms as a tea tray, which I have decided to hold between my thighs. The tray would so easily tip, dropping its contents, but my task is to hold it horizontal. Similarly, the whole of the horse's forehand would like to tip, but the rider's thighs must hold it up. If the horse can persuade you to lean back and stretch your leg down so that you tip the carousel pole, he has all the room he needs to

**Photo 6.9**
This is the same phase in the canter stride that we saw in Photo 6.1, but Dancer is much less overbent, and Diane's upper body is shorter, with her ribs dropped down more towards her hips, and the front angle between her thigh and torso more closed.

drop his tea tray. In **Photo 6.1** Dancer has done this to Diane, and her correction must hold that front angle much more closed, as she is doing in **Photo 6.9**. To do this she has to keep her front tendons up, as Jo learned in Chapter 4 (**Photo 4.8**, page 79). The correction has undoubtedly made a difference, although it had less effect on Dancer than the equivalent correction in trot. The bottom line is that she needs to risk feeling weirder than her wildest dreams, and to do it *more*.

However, this is easier said than done, and since the horse's forehand naturally rocks down in canter, his movement tips and rocks the rider's carousel pole more than the more level movement of trot. So unless the canter is naturally of a really high quality, the issues of falling on the forehand and overbending are frequently more challenging. They put the rider slap-bang into the 'catch 22' that we met in the earlier chapters: until she sits right, the horse cannot go right, but until the horse goes right, she cannot sit right. Thus a diving horse creates a rocking rider, and a rocking rider creates a diving horse. But since the horse has no investment in changing the pattern, it has to be the rider who somehow becomes more still, leading them both – we hope – from a vicious to a virtuous circle.

The better the canter, the easier it is to sit still, but the rider will almost always have a slight rock. Her aim, as we saw in the chapter on Heather, is to

**Photo 6.10**
There is every chance here that Diane will stop herself from leaning back and stop Dancer from overbending as they reach the third beat of the canter stride.

make it go from vertical to forward, with the forward rock happening as the horse's hind legs come under him and his forehand lifts. You can think of this as a miniature version of the fold down that you make as the horse takes off for a jump. In the second and third beats of the stride the rider attempts to stay vertical, refusing to lean back and open that front angle. **Photo 6.10** is taken slightly earlier in the stride than **Photos 6.1** or **6.9**, and it looks as though Diane will certainly avoid the rock back of **Photo 6.1**, and may well hold her torso – and her horse – in a better place than she did in **Photo 6.9**. By holding up the tea tray she is using her thighs as if she could lever the front of the saddle up off the horse – except that, in reality, *they lever the horse's forehand up with it.*

This lesson provides a beautiful illustration of my favourite question: does the organised rider organise the disorganised horse, or does the disorganised horse disorganise the organised rider? It is no mean achievement to anchor the carousel pole so well that instead of the horse tipping and rocking you about, you can lever up his forehand and change the quality of his movement. While I was writing this chapter, a more organised Diane emailed me from Germany, talking about the lesson she had on the day she flew there. This developed the same theme. 'It was well worth the effort,' she wrote, 'and the focus on lengthening that area under the left side of my seat was very helpful. I have a fancy young three-year-old stallion and it makes all the difference in the world when I am going left. Even though I did it unconsciously to a degree before, I can now more easily pick up my horses with my seat, know how to do it, and focus on doing it …'. She has more tools in her rider's tool kit, and an understanding of cause and effect which I would like more riders to share.

# CHAPTER 7

# Symmetry and the turning aids | Sue

BEFORE THE SESSION THAT YOU SEE HERE Sue had taken several lessons with Denise, one of the senior coaches of my work, whom you will meet later. So she had already had some exposure to this style of coaching. I had been searching for a rider whose torso made a 'C' curve to the right, and I wanted someone who had done enough of the basic work that I could go straight into working with this issue, tackling it for the first time. Denise knew just the person, so I invited Sue to take part.

Sue's mare Ella is now nine, and Sue bought her as a five-month-old foal. Both parents are Hanoverian/Thoroughbred crosses, and there is a hint of Irish Draught at the level of her maternal grandfather. Mentally, however, her Thoroughbred genes seem to dominate. Sue hacks Ella out, and has competed her in various riding club competitions, including dressage and showing; but like so many riders at the 'grass roots' level of the sport, she has not attempted the affiliated levels. Sue realises that her horse has much more potential than she has ever brought out, and in her most despairing moments she has wondered if she should sell her to a more experienced and skilled rider. She finds Ella tricky enough to ride at home, but to compound her sense of inadequacy, the mare is even more difficult to ride at a competition.

Contrary to many people's suppositions, horses do not stand in the field or stable feeling full of angst that they have not yet reached Medium (Third), or any other level; their main requirements are to be well fed and fairly treated. Undoubtedly, Ella is a talented horse who could go far with the right rider; but it is my opinion that Sue should keep her, and should ideally invest in some short spells where she is worked by someone more skilful. In the UK, few riders have enough disposable income to keep their horse permanently in training, and even when the money is available, I am not convinced that this is the best way to learn.

Sue needs the help of someone who can change the horse's way of going just enough to give her the chance to step out of the 'catch 22' of riding. This states

**Photo 7.1**
Ella is pushing back at Sue early on in the lesson, but she has not become too disorganised.

that until Sue sits right the horse will not go right, but until the horse goes right Sue cannot sit right. A more correctly moving horse presents Sue with a window of opportunity, but the window will remain open only if Sue's body can then match the 'rightness' of that new pattern. Otherwise, the horse will soon revert back to the pattern that matches Sue's less correct 'bumprint'. This could leave Sue feeling demoralised (especially if it happens repeatedly), so ideally the horse should be patterned to a level just slightly above the level of Sue's riding. This gives her the best chance of catching up to the horse. But if Ella is ridden by a more elite rider, Sue will not stand a chance of matching the correctness of that 'bumprint'. Ironically, this often compounds the rider's problems, since the horse is now armed with some new comparisons which show her just how un-skilled her rider really is!

In previous chapters we have looked at the four main defaults, addressing the issues created by the rider/horse interaction on the planes of back/front and up/down. We are now looking at the side/side plane, which, for many riders, presents a new and more intractable default than the other planes. Splitting them up like this is just a way to simplify our thinking; in reality, they all affect each other. But without some prior work on the rider's main default and the issues presented in the previous chapters, it is difficult to get her to the point where she has enough 'brainspace' to take on an asymmetry correction, let alone the ability to make it stick.

**Photo 7.1** shows an early moment on the left rein in trot, where Ella has pushed back at Sue and hollowed her back; but Sue is coping well, and is doing her utmost to make her push forward bigger than the horse's push back. She is also attempting to 'kneel' her way out of the horse's 'man-trap', and while her back looks slightly hollow, it is not obvious whether this, and/or tipping forward, was her original default. It does, however, look highly unlikely that she leant back or rounded her back. By **Photo 7.2** she has succeeded rather well, and

**Photo 7.2**
Here on the left rein Sue has made a significant improvement in Ella's carriage. She is not very stuffed but she is now reaching into the rein.

while Ella really needs more stuffing and is not yet tracking up, it is no mean achievement to improve the trot in such a short time from the beginning point of **Photo 7.1** to the trot of **Photo 7.2**.

However, on the right rein, the same degree of push-back causes much more distortion in Sue's body, and presents her with a far harder problem to solve. **Photo 7.3** (overleaf) shows how Sue's collapse to the right is a 'C' curve that shortens the right side of her torso and brings her chin to the right of the horse's midline. Look at the creases in her fleece, and also at the white line on it, which should be horizontal (as it clearly was in **Photo 7.1**). You can also see how her right elbow is all but resting on her right thigh. However, in the photographs taken on the left rein, her left elbow was about level with the point of her hip. Her right hand has crossed the horse's neck and is behind her left hand – and the way that her stick lies over the very top of her thigh is a knock-on effect that is far from ideal.

While **Photo 7.3** clearly shows the side bend of the 'C' curve, **Photo 7.4** (also overleaf) shows that there is also a twist in Sue's torso, which follows the extreme turn of her head to the right. Chiropractors and osteopaths tell us that a side bend is always accompanied by a twist, and this advances the shoulder on the side the person is twisting away from. Test this idea as you are sitting in your chair, and notice which side you naturally want to lean and twist to. How strange does it feel if you make the same gesture to the other side? The muscles of your sides, between your ribs and hips, will make creases on one side much more naturally than they will on the other, and this difference – between the side where the twist feels like 'home' and the side where it feels alien – will tell you your own default. This is highly likely to be a fatal flaw, for our asymmetry default is so much a part of who we are that as we travel through the layers of

**Photo 7.3**
On the right rein the same degree of push back disorganises Sue much more as it plays into her asymmetry. Notice Sue's right hand almost crosses Ella's neck, and how her right elbow all but rests on her right thigh. The white stripe on her fleece that should be horizontal drops down on the right.

**Photo 7.4**
This shows how Sue is looking to the right, with her whole torso twisted to the right. Her right hand is behind her left, and her right foot is way ahead of the ideal line.

the onion, the best we can do is to unravel it in stages. In most cases, it never leaves us; but we can learn to mitigate its effects.

The chances are that as you lean and twist, the seat bone on the side you are twisting towards becomes heavier while the other becomes lighter, and the more profound the twist, the more the advancing outside shoulder makes the outside seat bone lift and advance. By the time you are on a horse and dealing with the forces of his movement, as well as the forces that act on a circle, it does not take much of a lean and twist for that outside seat bone to disappear completely. Virtually everybody I teach begins with at least a 60:40 discrepancy in the weight on each seat bone when they are just walking the horse on a straight line, and getting from here to 50:50 is a big deal. But if you begin, as Sue did, with an 80:20 discrepancy, you are going to be in for a hard time. Knowing the dynamics of twists, leans and seat bones as intimately as I do, I insist that the riders aim to *keep equal weight on each seat bone in all of the movements*. When elite riders talk of weighting their inside seat bone more, I suspect that they are actually feeling more *tone* in the inside of their torso, but are mistaking this for more *weight*. Or perhaps their description is based less on feel than on the assumptions of the conventional wordscape.

A small percentage of riders, including Page who you will meet in Chapter 9, manage to make a side bend while riding in which they lift the inside seat bone, drawing it up towards the shoulder that is being drawn down. But Sue is showing us the most common pattern, which is actually shared by Carol, Jo, and Millie. In Sue it is particularly marked, causing that exaggerated way of looking, leaning and twisting to the right. The way her right hand is behind her left provides another clue, and as a result of the twist we see more of her front than her back. This becomes obvious if you compare **Photo 7.4** with **Photo 7.2**. Both are taken pretty much from the centre point of the circle Sue is riding; but on the left rein we see her in profile, while on the right we see more of her chest.

Notice too that in **Photo 7.4**, and also in **Photo 7.3**, Sue's inside (right) leg has come forward of the ideal hip/heel line. As the rider's outside shoulder comes forward, so, usually, does the inside leg, and as this happens Sue feels that she has no control of it; however hard she tries, she cannot keep it back underneath her. The more heavily weighted her inside seat bone becomes (taking some of the weight that ideally would still be on her outside (left) seat bone) the more up and forward her inside knee comes, and the less she can 'kneel' down that inside (right) thigh. She cannot reposition her leg until she can get weight off that inside seat bone and back onto the outer one. And she cannot do *that* until her outside shoulder comes back, which requires her to untwist herself and 'un-side-bend' herself. Although many trainers imply that this should be easy, the reality is a different story!

In your washing machine, the centrifugal force of the spin cycle pins your washing to the outside of tub. The same force is acting on Sue's backside (her centre of gravity) and sending it to the outside as her shoulders come to the inside. To realise why this force affects Sue on the right rein and not on the left, remember the idea of the spine being like a mast that is held in place by guy ropes. Those guy ropes are pre-set in a rotation and a lean to the right. The muscles of the sides of Sue's torso, and also the muscles of both thighs and calves have different tone, pulling on the skeleton in different ways. This twist determines how she walks around, sits at her desk, and lies in bed. Unless it gives her back or joint pain it might seem to be of little consequence; but once she gets on a horse, it matters.

In **Photo 7.4**, Ella's head is to the inside, with the bit pulled through her mouth. If Sue were not beside a fence/wall/edge/barrier and she was attempting to turn like this, she would pull Ella's head to go to the inside (right), but would not bring her wither or her body to the right. Not all riders realise that the head and the wither always go in opposite directions, and when riders lose control of the steering what usually happens is that the wither starts to act as a hinge, just like the hinge in an articulated lorry (eighteen wheeler). The horse's body then follows his wither, so as his head comes too much to the inside, the wither goes to the outside and the horse falls out on the circle. In the opposite scenario, the head goes out as the wither and body fall in, making the circle smaller. The key to steering lies in *not letting the wither act as a hinge*, and this means that pulling on the rein is not allowed.

There is a certain instinctive logic to the idea that pulling the right rein will make the horse go right, and pulling on the left rein will make him go left. But no one in their right mind would attempt to turn a bicycle by pulling on the inside handlebar, or to turn a wheelbarrow by pulling on the inside handle. If you made that mistake once, you would never make it again! Yet riders persist in attempting to turn by pulling on the inside rein, even though they have demonstrated time and time again that doing this jack-knifes the horse even more, getting them into even deeper trouble as he falls out on the circle. In the inverse of this problem, riders pull on the outside rein to try to stop the horse falling in, only to find that he falls in even more as he jack-knifes even more... (See **Fig. 7.1**)

Those instinctive attempts to steer will quickly put horse and rider into the spiral of increasing tension, as Sue demonstrates well. The more she tries to solve her steering problem by pulling on the inside rein, the more she scrunches

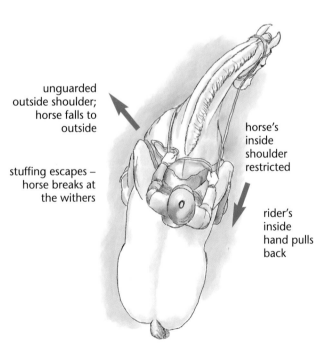

**Fig. 7.1**
The rider attempts to steer to the right by pulling on the inside (right) rein. As her right hand comes back so does her right shoulder, so her whole torso rotates with her left shoulder and hand advancing. This gives the horse an escape route for his outside (left) shoulder. The wither acts as a hinge and he jack-knifes, falling out on the circle.

unguarded outside shoulder; horse falls to outside

stuffing escapes – horse breaks at the withers

horse's inside shoulder restricted

rider's inside hand pulls back

the inside of the horse, making the horse push back at her more on that side. We see this in **Photo 7.4**: as Sue's hand pulls back, the twist brings her inside shoulder back and makes her heavy inside seat bone fall even further back down the horse's 'man-trap'. Thus the inside of the horse hollows away from that weighted seat bone. As Ella hollows more she pushes back at Sue more. This makes her harder to turn, and makes Sue pull back more. Sue's body so easily falls into pulling, collapsing and twisting – and as the horse falls into jack-knifing, hollowing, and pushing back, they 'wind each other up'. But on the other rein Sue can resist both the force of the horse's push-back and the centrifugal force with far less problem – and thanks to her guy ropes her body stays on the correct axis without her having to think about it.

As Sue delves deeper into the layers of the onion she will one day discover that her left side is advanced too much while it is on the inside of the left rein circle. But for now, this presents such a small problem relative to her difficulties on the right rein that she simply perceives the left rein as 'good'! The problems of turning evolve as one solves them layer by layer; but the most enduring factor is that pulling on the inside rein is the default option for the rider who has lost control of her seat bones and torso. What you need is *something else to do instead of pulling*, and that something must address the causes of the problem (i.e. the disappearing seat bone and the deformation of the torso) and not its symptom (i.e. the overwhelming desire to pull).

There are a number of variations on the theme of how people are taught to turn a horse. They involve 'this hand here and that leg there', and the pelvis and shoulders pointing in various directions. But in my experience, all of them miss the point, and rather than voicing the arguments, I am going to cut through them by drawing an analogy to ice-skating. When an ice-skater travels on an arc of a circle, she pushes off her outside foot and glides on her inner one. The most important observation is that her body faces to the outside of the circle – and if she twists it to face inwards, she spirals outwards and loses control of the turn. The same laws of physics are acting on horses and their riders, and in **Photos 7.2** and **7.4** we are seeing their effects. Twist to the inside, and you are doomed to pull on the inside rein as you contort the horse's body and lose control of the turn. Keep your torso on the radius of the circle, and your horse turns just like that wheelbarrow.

If this seems like heresy, I recommend watching the world's most skilled riders, and paying attention – without any preconceived ideas – to what they actually do. Sue's asymmetry beautifully illustrates the most common pattern, although there are many variations on the theme, and some riders show a pattern in which the attempt to solve the original problem has become the new problem! For example, think of a rider making a 'C' curve like Sue, who is then told to drop her outside shoulder. If this is all she does, her spine deforms into an 'S' shape, displacing her ribcage like one of the moves in 'break-dance'. Try it yourself so you really understand! (See **Fig. 7.2** overleaf.)

Before **Photo 7.5** (also overleaf) was taken I brought Sue's legs up over the

**Fig. 7.2**
Rider (a) has the same problem as Sue, but if someone tells her to fix it by dropping her outside shoulder she will develop an 'S' curve instead of a 'C' curve to her spine, like the rider in (b). The attempt to solve the problem will have become the new problem!

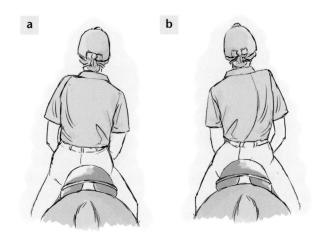

**Photo 7.5**
I am attempting to get Sue to 'kneel' more down her right thigh, so that her knee comes down and her foot comes back.

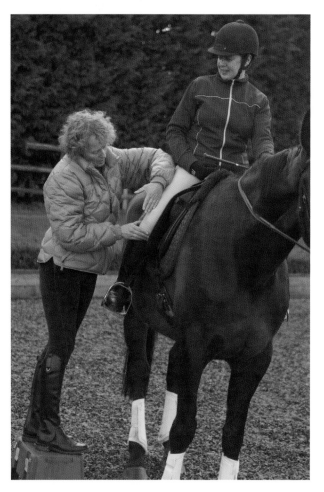

front of the saddle and repositioned them as I did with Carol in Chapter 3. I then checked her understanding of bear down, and I am now explaining how she needs to 'kneel' more down her right thigh, keeping her knee down and her foot back. It is helpful to think of the seat bone and the knee being at opposite ends of the diameter of a wheel. (See **Fig. 7.3**) Sue's asymmetry turns that wheel so that as her seat bone becomes heavier, her knee comes up; so we have to lighten that inside seat bone in order to turn the wheel the other way and bring her knee down. I suggested that Sue thought of aiming her right point of hip towards her horse's left ear, as this makes the seat bone lighten and the wheel turn. But the other side of the coin is that we also have to find the left seat bone and keep it weighted.

As Sue's lean and twist bring her chin to the right, so her backside drifts to the left, and her left seat bone falls away from the horse's midline. Since this puts it on a lower part of the saddle, it is perfectly logical that she cannot feel it clearly or keep weight on it. Slipping to the left is also part of the dynamic that brings Sue's right knee up, and for a dramatic understanding of this, imagine falling off with your backside sliding to the left. You could perhaps rescue yourself as long as your right knee had come no further up than the pommel, but if you sustained a position like this, imagine how hard your right thigh would work to hold you on! While Sue's right inner thigh muscles are working extremely hard, her left thigh is cruising.

You see the slide of Sue's backside to the left in **Photo 7.6**, although if she were in motion, and were really ex-

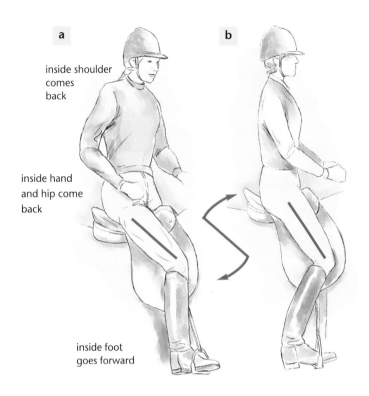

a

inside shoulder
comes
back

inside hand
and hip come
back

inside foot
goes forward

b

**Fig. 7.3**
In (a) the rider is twisted to the right like Sue. Her right seat bone is back and heavy, and her right knee comes up with her foot forward. If she aims her right point of hip towards the horse's left ear she advances and lightens the right seat bone, and this rotates her thigh bone into the correct place. This brings the knee and foot back, as if the thigh bone were the diameter of a wheel.

In (b) the rider has used this rotation to realign herself so that her hands are level, we see her in profile, and she has a shoulder/hip/heel vertical line.

**Photo 7.6**
As we look at Sue from the back, we can see the creases which shorten the right side of her torso. Her head is tilted to the right, and if she were riding on a circle to the right the forces acting on her body would make her lean to the right even more. Concurrently her backside is displaced to the left, so that it hangs off the left side of the saddle.

periencing the effects of the centrifugal force, the curve in her spine would put her chin and shoulders more to the right. So the photograph is slightly misleading; but we can still see the creases in the right side of her waist area, and her head tilted to the right. The slip of her backside to the left becomes obvious when you realise how much of her backside and thigh are visible to the left of the saddle, and how little they are visible to the right of it. (Unfortunately the photograph was not taken directly from the back, but this is barely distorts our view.) In **Photo 7.7** (overleaf) I have my hands around Sue's left side, in the angle where her torso meets her thigh, and I have suggested that she imagines riding on the right rein as I stand in the centre of the circle, holding a lunge rein which passes around her just here. The pull I maintain on that lunge rein stops her backside sliding off to the left.

As I put my hands on Sue in **Photo 7.7**, she suddenly felt her left seat bone much more clearly. The pressure of my hands drew it towards the horse's midline, and as a result her torso lined up vertically, with even creases in her fleece, and her chin over the horse's midline. My hands in **Photo 7.7** also made Sue realise how much her left thigh had come away from the saddle, and **Photo**

**Photo 7.7**

As I put my hands in the crease where Sue's thigh meets her torso, I am asking her to imagine that I placed a lunge rein around her here. If I stood in the centre of her circle to the right and kept a tension in that lunge rein, I would pull her left side and seat bone towards the mid-line of the saddle. This would help her to weight that seat bone and keep her torso vertical.

**7.8** (opposite) shows a wonderful way to address the difference in the tone of the inner thigh muscles. Sue has made her right hand into a fist, and has placed her knuckles on the saddle just in front of her right thigh. As she pushes her fist against the saddle she can use that counter-pressure to push her opposite thigh against the saddle, and she can target just the muscles she needs, without involving the muscles of her right thigh which are already far stronger.

Sue was shocked to discover how much her left seat bone and left thigh had slid away to the left – although they had, in fact, been giving her horse permission to slide off to the left as well! Meanwhile, her right thigh had taken on the job of stopping her backside from sliding off completely. None of this had been part of Sue's perception of a problem that she had attributed to her errant right hand and her difficult horse. So as she walked on again, she was able to imagine the lunge rein and the feeling of my hands, and to put her inside fist on the side of the pommel whenever necessary. These ideas were intended to help her keep equal weight on each seat bone, and to keep them equally close to the horse's spine with both thighs equally firmly on the saddle. I also kept asking her to glance down at the horse's mane and to notice if her chin was over it or off to the right. If she could keep the seat bone and the chin in place, she had much more chance of 'kneeling' down her right thigh and maintaining the shoulder/hip/heel alignment on her right side.

If Sue is to stop herself from leaning to the right she has to stop herself from twisting to the right as well. In order to position her torso like the ice-skater, she has to think of looking to the outside (left), even though she is turning right – but this is no handicap as her peripheral vision easily enables her to see where she is going. The correct position of her torso can also be described as a right-handed fencing lunge, and our correction of aiming her inside hip towards the horse's outside ear also helps with this. As the rider's inside hip advances so her outside shoulder comes back, spiralling the body in the opposite direction to the pull of her guy ropes. This helps to keep her inside hand giving forward. At the same time, as we showed in **Fig. 7.3**, she has lightened the inside seat bone and turned the wheel of the inside thigh in the right direction. But as shown in

**Fig. 7.4** (overleaf) these corrections can present the rider with a dramatic feeling of being twisted to the outside. The reality is that her original 'home' was twisted, but she could not 'smell' the contortion that was so, so familiar. The irony is that I have straightened her out – but in the process, I have made her feel twisted. Sue's lesson had begun to offer her a massive dose of 'weird'!

The bottom line is that if she is not to fall into the default of pulling on the inside rein, she has to pay attention to her body and hold it in the best alignment she can muster, noticing in each moment how this affects the horse. She has to discover what she gets when she gets it, and what she loses when she loses it. Thus she

Photo 7.8
Sue has made a fist out of her right hand and has placed her knuckles against the side of the pommel. As she presses against the saddle she can also press her left thigh and seat bone against it, bringing them more towards the midline. This strengthens the weaker muscles on her left side.

gradually begins to 'reinvent the wheel' of the turning aids, discovering what others have discovered before her. Riders soon begin to figure out that if the wither is not to act as a hinge, and the horse is not to turn like an articulated lorry, he has to turn instead like a bus. This means that the whole of his front end turns around his back end, rather like a turn on the haunches.

The trick to this is that the outside of the horse must not be allowed to get too long. If the rider can keep her chin over the horse's mane and maintain ice-skating or fencing-lunge position, then her outside seat bone can stay far back and close to the horse's spine while carrying fifty per cent of her weight. Concurrently her outside shoulder stays back, her outside elbow stays back and her outside hand stays back – as if her outside aids make a wall. Remember that she must not turn as if pulling on the inside handlebar of the bicycle, and that if the inside handlebar comes back, the outside one comes forward! So the wall of her outside aids closes the gap that the wither would fall through, and keeps the outside of the horse short. At the same time, it is helpful to think of the inside of the horse staying long, for if he hinges at the wither, it will shorten too much. It helped Sue to think of counter-flexing her horse, but it is not that we actually want him to look to the outside; it is just that we do not want him to look to the inside.

Again, this may sound like heresy, and confusion arises because many riders who are jack-knifing their horses are extremely proud of their bend to the inside. Yes, they can see their horse's inside eye, but they seem oblivious to the

**Fig. 7.4**
With crookedness in particular, you subjective feelings are not to be trusted. When you counteract your natural asymmetry, you will feel as if you have brought your outside seat bone and shoulder so far back that you are facing way too much to the outside.

(a) The rider who is crooked to the right is actually placed like this…

(b)…but she feels symmetrical

(c)… when her shoulders and pelvis lie on the radius of the circle she is riding she will feel like this.

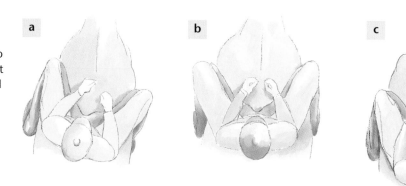

fact that they have completely lost control of his wither! A jack-knife is not a bend, and before you can find out what a bend really is, you have to learn to steer the wither and to keep the horse straight. This means that his body is always moving on a tangent of the circle. Think of the circle as an eight- or twelve-sided coin; to make each side you bring the wither to the inside, keeping the outside of the horse short and using the wall of the outside aids to block the escape route through which the wither might fall to the outside. If you do this well enough, you find that you can give away your inside hand as your horse moves happily around on the circle.

As I am sure you have realised, steering is a complicated dynamic, because everything is dependent on everything else, and if you lose one piece in the puzzle you lose the whole lot! Whenever we move from the issues of back/front and up/down into the issues of side/side, we open Pandora's box, and even a simple

**Photo 7.9**
On the right rein in walk Sue is doing well. She is no longer rotated to the right, her hands are level, and she is much closer to the ideal shoulder/hip/heel vertical line. Ella is reaching well into the rein.

explanation requires the rider to take in a lot of information. Inevitably she will not have enough awareness to track everything, so we have to find the 'triggers' that work best for her, linking the wordscape to the brainscape and giving her the greatest possible improvement. Sue had to think particularly of looking left, keeping that outside seat bone in place, and bringing her inside hip towards the horse's outside ear. In **Photo 7.9** she is setting everything up in walk on the right rein, and is doing pretty well, with a good response from Ella. Notice that the bit is not pulled through her mouth to the right – a tell-tale sign that often persists even when the rider thinks she has solved the problem. But our transition to trot, a moment later, led to the disaster of **Photo 7.10.** I have included this just to give heart to anyone who has experienced the same problem. When your schooling session feels like a game of 'Snakes and Ladders' you and the horse are obviously not having the ideal experience; but your only choice is to go back to walk, set things up all over again, and attempt to keep both the horse's attention and your own alignment throughout your next transition!

In **Photo 7.11** (shown overleaf) Sue is doing much better. We see her more in profile, her hands are level, and there is more distance between her elbow and her thigh – although I suspect that her right side still has some creases, and that her left seat bone has drifted off to the left. She is still looking to the right, and is not quite managing to 'kneel' enough down her right leg, although in **Photo 7.12** (also overleaf) she has changed this. Ella is not reaching into the rein quite so well and she has her mouth open, but Sue is holding her alignment well. We see her in profile, and for the first time her chin is not leading her torso into that rotation right.

I was very pleased that Sue's clinic gave her a run of five lessons and five supervised practice sessions, giving her more time to take in the whole picture and also to discover (as it were) the first domino to fall each time that she lost

**Photo 7.11**
Here in trot Sue is doing much better. Although she is still looking to the right we see her torso in profile, but she is not yet 'kneeling' enough down her right leg.

**Photo 7.12**
Ella is not reaching into the rein quite as well as she was in Photo 7.11, but Sue has kept her shoulders and pelvis on the radius of the circle she is riding and she is 'kneeling' more effectively down her right thigh. Her reins are dangerously long.

it. We all have unequal guy ropes and distortions in our torso, which form a fundamental part of the 'bumprint' that patterns our horses. None of us can ever afford to stop working on our asymmetry, and it can be very humbling to realise that what you had considered an 'evasion' that had nothing to do with you actually had everything to do with you. It was simply the horse's reflection of your 'bumprint'.

# CHAPTER 8

# Stacking the torso | Karin

KARIN FIRST CAME ON ONE OF MY COURSES in 2000. As a teenager she had evented her horse to Intermediate level and passed her British Horse Society Assistant Instructor's examination, and after attending a number of ridden and teacher training courses with me, she became accredited as a Ride With Your Mind Coach. She then taught a few freelance clients alongside her job in marketing. But two years ago she was made redundant, and since then she has been working freelance, mostly in the village where I live. She teaches, fills in as a groom, and helps me run my business.

Karin's success in her teens was remarkable given that it came after an injury that would have stopped less determined souls. As a youngster she was a competitive swimmer, and one morning after a gruelling training session, she woke up to find that she could not move her left leg. By that afternoon she was in hospital in traction, where she remained for the next two weeks. While movement and feeling did come back into her leg, she was left with back pain that often had her in tears. She gave up swimming, but against her doctor's orders she refused to give up riding, and she was relieved to find that even when she was eventing seriously, it reduced the pain.

However, it is only in the last few years that she has really found relief. Curiosity led her to attend 'Awareness Through Movement' classes, which are part of the Feldenkrais Method of movement re-education. Inspired by their effect on her, Karin has trained as a Feldenkrais teacher, and she now offers classes and individual sessions to the riders who come on my courses. Being able to work with their physical issues off horse is tremendously helpful to them (whether or not they are in pain), for even those of us without apparent problems benefit from moving beyond the habitual patterns which limit our freedom of movement.

For this lesson Karin rode Astro, one of the school horses at my home base, Overdale Equestrian Centre at Nether Westcote in the Cotswold Hills. He is a fourteen-year-old Danish warmblood, who was given to us several years ago. His

**Photo 8.1**
As Karin rides away from the camera on the left rein we see that her spine and head make a 'C' curve to the left. Her backside, however, remains in the centre of the saddle, unlike Sue's.

**Photo 8.2**
From the inside of the circle we see how the lean of Photo 8.1 also involves a twist which brings Karin's left hand back. Thus we see more of her chest than her back. Unusually, her left lower leg is too far back.

owner was paying very expensive livery for him on the fringes of London, and when she could not sell him she decided to cut her losses. I do not know his history, but suspect that someone 'laid into' what they thought was a fine young horse who was shirking his duty. But actually they were beating a very weak young horse who was physically much less capable than he looked. He subsequently lost any desire to co-operate, and when he arrived at Overdale his favourite occupation was standing in the middle of the arena and kicking out with one hind leg every time he was asked to move. Now, however, he is quite forward-going in the school.

I particularly wanted Karin to take part in this project because of her asymmetry. The injury she suffered has inevitably left its mark, and she has a very obvious rotation to the left – the less common side. Over the last few years she has been peeling away its layers, both through her riding and through her Feldenkrais training, and these have combined to accelerate her progress, and also to give her an enhanced awareness of her body. **Photo 8.1** shows her riding away from the camera in trot on the left rein, and although the centre of her backside is in the centre of the saddle (unlike Sue's in **Photo 7.6**) her spine clearly makes a 'C' curve to the left, putting her chin to the left of the horse's midline.

Seen from the inside, this creates the picture of **Photo 8.2**. Karin is unusual in that as she rotates to the left her inside leg comes back. She suspects that her twist to the left was honed during her teens, when her job in the local riding school involved teaching lessons. In these she rode a horse along the local country lanes while leading a pony – but those recalcitrant ponies kept dragging her left side backwards! While Karin's lower leg is atypical, the rest of her pattern *is* typical in that you clearly see her left hand behind her right, with the bit pulled slightly through the horse's mouth to the left. You also see more of her chest than her back.

**Photo 8.3** shows trot on the right rein, and although it was taken very early in her session, Karin is doing well. In trot, she makes Astro look relatively easy to ride, and it is in canter that she struggles more with a push back that can be much bigger than you might imagine from these photographs. (**Photos 8.4, 8.7** and **8.8** might give you the idea of how well Astro can imitate a giraffe!) In **Photo 8.3** Karin's shoulders are raised slightly, and it would be better if her elbows were more bent. Her right hand may still be slightly in advance of her left, and although Astro's mouth is slightly open, the bit is not pulled through it. The bottom line is that Karin never finds herself tempted to pull on the right rein like she is tempted to pull on the left, and it is no coincidence that we see much less of her chest than we do on the left rein. This shows us that her torso is now on the radius of the circle she is riding, so she is not rotated to the inside as she is when tracking left. Her inside (right) leg could be very slightly more back under her, and ideally her foot would be flat (if not heel down); but it still looks stronger and more stuffed than her left leg, which, as shown in **Photo 8.2**, is almost always on tip-toe.

Canter, as a faster and inherently asymmetrical gait, always makes asymmetry patterns come to the fore, but it also often amplifies the issues of the up/down and back/front planes. Our early lessons tend to focus mostly on work in trot, so the rider's skills in canter may lag behind her trot work (and each of us is, by definition, going to find one of the gaits more difficult than the other). **Photo 8.4** (overleaf) shows left canter early on in the session, and Karin has reverted to her original default, hollowing her back and lifting her chin. Astro has done the same, and we have to address his push–back before we can look at the issues of the side/side plane. However, I suspect that Karin's chin is still to the

Photo 8.3
On the right rein we see Karin's torso in profile. Her right foot would ideally be slightly more back under her with more 'kneel' down her right thigh. Astro is beginning to reach into the rein, although his legs do not make a symmetrical 'M' shape. Until the advancing legs reach more forward he will be on his forehand.

127

**Photo 8.4**
In canter left Karin is struggling. She has hollowed her back, and bought her left hand down towards her left thigh, bringing it back behind her right hand. Astro has also hollowed, and he is not turning well.

inside of Astro's midline. Notice how her left hand is practically resting on her left thigh, while her right hand is way more forward and higher up; this is symptomatic of a 'handlebar turn'.

When Astro pushes back at Karin in right canter, as shown in **Photo 8.5**, she becomes far less disorganised: her reins are too long with her hands too close to her body, but she still looks strong, reasonably well lined up, and in profile. A stronger bear down and more 'kneeling' out of Astro's 'man-trap' will solve this problem relatively easily, as they have in **Photo 8.6**. Karin has lost control of her lower leg, however, with her toe turning out, and it would be better if her backside were more in the saddle. Many riders find that the back of their backside peels away from the saddle in canter (probably much more than this), and I often find that they can fix this really well if I suggest that they think of attaching themselves to the horse from further back on their pelvic floor.

When riders bump in canter they do not leave the saddle with the whole of their underneath, as they do in trot. Many riders pivot around a point on their inner thigh as their calves, knees and torso all rock back and forth, and this causes the back of their backside to leave the saddle. In a large bump only their pubic bone stays attached; with less of a bump their seat bones might stay attached, but the organised rider stays attached all the way back to her butt crack.

**Photo 8.5**
In canter right we again see Karin in profile. Astro is still hollow and pushing back, but Karin is not too disorganised by this. Her reins are too long.

Photo 8.6
Astro is beginning to reach into the rein. Karin's reins are a better length, but she has lost control of her lower leg, which clings on to Astro's side as her toe turns out.

Thinking of this helps the rider stay attached to the saddle better than anything else I know! Heather shows us in **Photos 2.9–2.12** how her canter seat includes a slight rock forward of her torso, which keeps her backside in contact with the saddle. Diane's backward rock also stops her from bumping, but it encourages her horse to dive onto his forehand. (**Photo 6.1**, page 97). The stiller the rider can sit, and the more she can attach her underneath to the horse, the more she can attach the horse to her, and the bigger the influence she has on him.

**Photos 8.7** and **8.8** show Karin demonstrating the difference between the full extent of her range when she twists to the left and the right. Her torso is rotated much more in the turn to the left, where on the right she primarily rotates her neck to look over her right shoulder. (You might want to try this while sitting in your chair, confirming the difference between your two sides.) On the left rein we have to stop this twist from happening – but it is so built in to her body

Photos 8.7–8.8
Karin shows the difference between the full extent of her range as she rotates to the left and the right. We see far more of her chest as she rotates to the left in Photo 8.7, but as she rotates to the right in Photo 8.8 she predominantly looks over her right shoulder.

Fig. 8.1
The lines of the
boards as they pass
over the rider's
back and front.

that strong antidotes are needed. As a mirror image of Sue, Karin has focused on keeping her right shoulder and right seat bone back to help her keep ice-skating or fencing-lunge position while riding on the left rein. It has also helped her to think of aiming her inside (left) hip towards the horse's outside ear. As you see in **Photo 8.1**, Karin has much more control of how her seat bones are placed and weighted than Sue has, and as a result she can keep her backside much more central. However, it is still difficult to keep her torso stacked up over that base.

A fundamental element of the progress she has made has been derived from the 'boards exercise', and I am going to suggest that you do this now, in your chair. I think the end result will shock you, *and I want you to have this shock,* because without it, my input is merely words. Even if you are finding this as enjoyable and fascinating as I would like you to, you are going no further than re-thinking the knowledge of your wordscape. There is much more value in

a

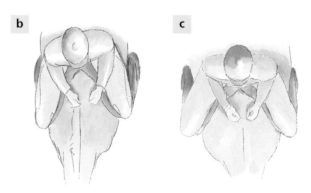

Fig. 8.2
(a) Advancing the right board to put it 'on' as it comes closer to the midline. The rider seen from above as in (b) advances that side of her torso. Thus having 'one board on' contributes to the rotation that is the cornerstone of most people's asymmetry. Having 'both boards on' brings the rider into the symmetrical position of (c).

b          c

connecting those words to your brainscape, and until you do this, you have no idea of what it takes to cross the gap between conceptual and working knowledge. Without this experience, you will never appreciate just what it takes to stabilise your torso and become a skilled rider.

So, sit in a hard chair with your seat bones pointing straight down, your feet flat on the floor, and your legs slightly apart. Instead of dividing the torso into halves, as we do if we think of the spine as its central axis, we are going to divide it into thirds. The lines that do this follow the line of a man's braces (suspenders), from a shoulder strap, over the bosom, down the edge of the abdominal muscle, continuing down to the corner of the pubic bone. On the back they follow those braces from the shoulder strap past the waist, down the line of the sacroiliac joint, and under the backside to the seat bone. Think of the lines on each side as the backs and fronts of two boards that pass through you, giving you a right third, a middle third, and a left third.

Put the edges of your hands on the front of one of the boards, lying them along the line from just beneath your bosom to the corner of your pubic bone. You are then going to make that line come closer to your midline; think of rotating your body slightly to advance that board (advancing its back as well), and imagine that if the third of your body to the outside of the board were full of stuffing, you are pushing the stuffing against the board in order to firm it up and move it over.

When you have done this, return to the neutral position, and notice that there is a symmetrical 'V' shape between your inner thighs, with the point of the 'V' towards the back of your underneath. Repeat the movement you made above, and notice how it changes that 'V'. One of its arms should become longer and stronger, with the other becoming shorter and fuzzier. Most people find that the side on which they advanced and clarified the board becomes longer, and that their thigh feels longer as well. If this is not the case, wait and see what happens as you do the same exercise on the other side.

So as you reverse sides, put your hands on the front of the other board, and move that towards your midline. Think of slightly advancing the third that lies outside it, and pushing its stuffing against the board. It is probably already clear to you that this side is different – it is highly likely that you instinctively chose your more functional side to start with, and that this side feels less convincing. Notice again how doing this changes the 'V' shape of your thighs. Having done the exercise on both sides, you can probably now make sure that the arm of the 'V' on the side you are advancing becomes longer and stronger. Practise on both sides as you need to.

If you were riding I would make you do this a number of times on each rein, suggesting that as you bring one board closer to the horse's midline, you let the other one deliberately come off, away from the horse's midline. I call this 'one side on, one side off' and most people soon realise that they do indeed ride like this, making one position an exaggeration of 'home', and the other one an alien place that is hard to get into. If one side is very much stronger than the other, you may find that it is just as difficult to get the stronger side to let go as it is to get the weaker side to engage; but it is important to work on this, or your strong side will continue to dominate. You may, however, show a different variation on the theme, perhaps with the top of one board being strong while the bottom of the other is strong. Or perhaps the tops and bottoms of both boards are reasonably strong, while both of their middles are soggy.

Once you have figured out how to make each board as good as you can right now, it is time for the punch-line. Whether you are on a chair or a on a horse, put on the board of the weaker, trickier side, and keep it in place as you then put on the other board too. As a pupil once suggested, putting 'both boards on' is reminiscent of two people both fighting to sit on the same bar stool, but neither one is allowed to push the other one off! Your middle third has been squashed from both sides and made narrower. It has become much less significant than the outer thirds, which are now held very firmly.

Sit like this for a while and notice that the 'V' between your thighs is again symmetrical, with both of its 'arms', as well as both of your thighs, becoming longer and stronger. *Breathe* in this position, and realise that you have no choice but to bear down, and that you would never sit in a chair (or 'just hang out') with this much tone in your torso! It is a completely unnatural way to sit – and you can work up quite a sweat while doing it – but it is a minimum requirement if you are to begin to move beyond the basics of riding.

I can practically hear the howls of disbelief. But you probably howled too when I first introduced the idea of bearing down, and I hope you are coming to terms with that now, and discovering what a huge difference it makes to your power, influence, and stability. Remember, too, how the skilled riders who insist that they are 'doing nothing' or simply 'relaxing', are really only telling you that they 'do not smell it any more'. If you dream of riding like Heather (or even if you only dream of one day riding shoulder-in), 'both boards on' has to become easy – a given – so that you can work on the layers of the onion that lie deeper than this, and that all contribute to your precision and influence as a rider.

Outrageous as it may seem at the moment, this can be done over time, and 'both boards on' can begin to feel far less stressful. It can even become 'home' – although it will never feel as normal on a chair as it does on a horse. As the strength and clarity of your boards increase over time, you will concurrently discover that it can take many years for them to reveal the soggy or missing segments that you were blissfully unaware of! Only a tiny percentage of riders naturally have 'both boards on', and even talented riders usually have a few aberrations that are having a significant effect on their horses.

When I wrote *Ride With Your Mind Masterclass* in 1991 I had not yet discovered the boards exercise. But I was working my way towards it, and trying to understand how and why the rider's 'good' and 'bad' reins would sometimes trade places. In my own riding, these changes drove me to distraction, but by 1995 I had the answer (and I wrote about the boards exercise in *For the Good of the Rider* and demonstrated it on the 'Rider's Guide to Body Awareness' videotape/DVD). *Everything I have learned since about turning, circling, straightness, bend, and lateral work* (which means all of the rider's expertise with side/side issues as explained in the rest of this book) *has been built on the baseline of the boards exercise.*

The bottom line is that without the narrowness which 'both boards on' brings to the rider's middle third, humans are too wide for horses, and one seat bone is bound to fall off the side of the horse. Like Sue, riders new to my work usually struggle to turn when the outside seat bone is falling off, and they cannot keep weight on it. They need to search for it (and then hold it) far back and close to the horse's spine, for only this enables them to maintain that fencing-lunge position, and to turn the horse like a bus. I often suggest that riders imagine sitting on a clock face, with twelve o'clock pointing towards the horse's head, and six o'clock pointing towards his tail. On the right rein, the outside (left) seat bone has to come back and in towards seven or eight o'clock, while on the left rein their outside (right) seat bone has to come back and in towards four or five o'clock. If they are positioned at nine or three, those outside seat bones will definitely go missing.

In each case the inside seat bone needs to be positioned on the opposite side of the clock to its partner, at ten past, or ten to the hour. Thinking like this is a great way to start working on the turning aids, but after a while, when riders have succeeded in getting their outside seat bone in place, they find that they suddenly cannot find their inside seat bone! This may create some small problems, but it is now on the other rein that the missing seat bone is on the outside, and this rein becomes the big deal. Since human beings are too wide for horses, 'One side on, one side off' can become a game of ping-pong between both seat bones and both reins that can last for a lifetime. And it can become highly frustrating and confusing.

To turn the horse effectively, the rider has to have *something to push round from* (i.e. the outside seat bone and board in the back position) and *something to push in to* (i.e. the inside seat bone, board, and thigh). It is as if the horse is a river, and the rider's body must provide both river banks, making a channel to funnel him through. She can then stop the horse's wither from acting as a hinge, and can stop herself from pulling on the inside rein. In an ideal world, steering the horse really does become as simple as steering a wheelbarrow – along goes his forehand in front of you, as if the reins were solid rods, and his

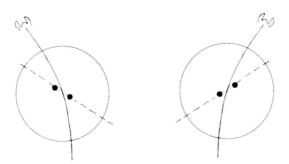

Fig. 8.3
On a circle the rider's seat bones are ideally equally weighted and positioned at ten to four on the left rein and ten past eight on the right rein. The exterior of the rider's body (i.e. her shoulders and pelvis) lie on the radius of the circle she is riding.

nose were the wheel.

However, the horse will not stop hingeing at the wither, unless both of the rider's seat bones lie on the inside edges of his long back muscles, i.e. the outside edges of the gullet of the saddle. This is the tough bit, which does not come naturally to anyone (not even Heather). 'Both boards on' makes it possible, and also lines the boards up over those edges, giving the rider a far more effective way to steer. But it also means (to put it bluntly) that she must not have any part of her anatomy down on the saddle in between her seat bones. They must be separated only by her butt crack. (How I wish someone had told me this years ago; it might have saved me from a huge amount of anguish, and from the difficulty of figuring it out!)

Remember the exercise I did with Sue (**Photo 7.8**, page 121), where she put her fist on the side of the pommel, and used the pressure of this to help her narrow in her opposite inner thigh and seat bone. This exercise has also helped Karin, who can position her seat bones much more precisely than Sue. If we can create a well-organised base, we at least have something to stack the torso up over, and we maximise our chances of creating a more symmetrical, functioning rider. **Photo 8.1** shows Karin doing a good job with each seat bone and the bottom of each board, but both of her boards curve to the left, and the lean and twist is stopping her from stacking up her entire torso.

The lean and twist also stop each of her outer thirds from being evenly stuffed. Karin has creases on her left side, which make that third 'soggy', and she has an overstretched right third, along with a higher right shoulder. Both sides need more stuffing, but the most obvious problem is on the left. When Karin attempts to put her left board on, she has to be careful not to make those left-side creases in the process; she has to imagine having a huge amount of stuffing in her left third, which keeps the edge of her body well away from the board even as the board gets firmer. If she is to lose those creases she also has to think about the position of her left shoulder, because the instant it goes to the

a           b

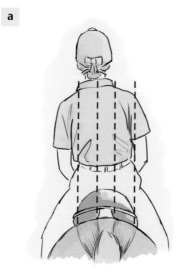 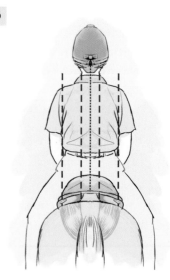

Fig. 8.4
In (a) the rider, like Karin, has a 'C' curve to the left, so she cannot stack her left epaulet and the whole of her left third over the horse's left long back muscle. Her right side, however, has almost remained stacked, unlike Karin's right side in Photo 8.1. In (b) both sides are stacked in the ideal way.

left, the creases reappear.

The idea of keeping her chin over the horse's mane is helpful, but it is even more helpful to think of the position of each 'epaulet'. Imagine a military or a doorman's uniform, where the epaulets are positioned at the top of each outer third. I like to ask the rider, 'Is your left epaulet stacked up over the horse's long back muscle as it lies underneath your left third and as it continues back behind you towards his croup? And is the right epaulet stacked up over the right side?' Almost always, one or both of them are not stacked up, and to help the rider stack them I put the palms of my hands against the backs of her hands and ask her to push her hands out against my resistance (**Fig. 8.5**). This defines the epaulets and the tops of the boards, and often makes it clear that one of her shoulders is in a distorted position. If we can correct this and organise the top of each third as well as organising the bottom, we have far more chance of organising the middle. When the rider is really well stuffed and stacked she is far more likely to have the influence she seeks.

As we have seen, a lean is always accompanied by a twist and Karin is not the only rider to have likened the untwisting of her torso to the turns that you make in a Rubik's cube as you line up its coloured segments. From a disorganised beginning she likes to think of the layers of her torso 'clicking' into place. In **Photo 8.8** both she and I have our hands on our ribcages, using them to rotate the midsection of the torso. This exercise is so powerful that before you do it you need to be sure that you know which way you tend to twist! Put your hand just below your bosom on the side you tend to twist towards, and then put your other hand against your ribs on the opposite side of your back. (You may find it easier to put your knuckles rather than your palm against your back.) Begin from a fencing-lunge position, which has advanced the side of your skeleton that tends to be rotated back. Then, think of your muscles forming a ring around your bones, and without moving your bones any further, use the pressure of your hands to move your muscles over your bones. It is as if your hands are saying 'All muscles responsible for rotation right (or left), *switch on now!*' You can make the same movement with your hands on the sides of your pelvis, and with them on your waist, giving you access to all three levels of the Rubik's cube. You may find that doing this helps you to feel the boards more clearly, clarifying their backs and fronts, and also the way that these line up in relation to each other as the board itself passes through you.

This exercise has really helped many people who felt that their rotation was an insurmountable force, and I wish I had thought of it years ago. I have watched so many riders struggle to maintain fencing-lunge position, and it is clear to me that doing this exercise makes it much more possible. (We call it 'The Chinese Burn', in memory of the big brothers and big bullies who inflicted tortuous twists on our arms when we were kids!) To many people, the feeling of the 'burn' is highly disorientating; but as their mind struggles to come to terms with it, they soon realise that the pay-off for this 'weirdness' (which builds on the idea of aiming the rider's inside hip towards the horse's outside

**Fig. 8.5**
If the rider pushes the backs of her hands outwards against the resistance of my hands, it helps her to feel and firm up the tops of the boards and thus to stack her epaulets.

**Photo 8.8**
Karin and I are doing the 'Chinese burn', putting pressure on the muscles of the torso so that we 'switch on' the muscles that create a rotation to the right, thus counteracting Karin's tendency to rotate to the left. This can be done on three levels of the torso.

**Photo 8.9**
I am giving Karin a resistance to push her left toe against, helping her to strengthen the muscles that will stop her lower leg from coming too far back.

ear) is far more control of both their body and their horse.

In **Photo 8.9** I have taken the idea a stage further by putting my hand in front of Karin's foot, and getting her to push the toe of her boot against my resistance. Her rotation is unusual in that her lower leg goes *back* on the side she rotates towards, and by pushing her toe forward against my resistance she increases the strength in the muscles of the front of her thigh and calf, which are weaker than those at the back. This push is a very neat way to mitigate her weakness. Sue, in contrast, showed us the more common pattern, with her lower leg going forward – and I could equally well have used a resistance with her, this time placing my hand *behind* her heel, having her push back into it. Again, this is a very clever and simple way to help her strengthen her weaker muscles, which are at the back of her thigh and calf.

**Photo 8.10** shows Karin in trot on the left rein. It is taken from a point on the radius of the circle she is riding, and we see her exactly in profile. Gone is the twist of **Photo 8.2**, in which we see the front of her torso and her inside (left) hand behind her outside (right) hand. Her lower leg is still a little dicey, her shoulders are slightly raised, and her inside wrist is turned over – but she is doing a good job despite these aberrations. Astro is no longer overbent, and is reaching well into the rein. He is not quite tracking up, so ideally Karin needs to send him more forward, but I suspect that she is struggling to hold everything together on the amount of power she currently has. Canter, too, is much improved, as shown in **Photo 8.11**, where the biggest issue is that Karin's reins are too long, bringing her hands too close to her body.

This lesson was, in reality, just another session in which Karin dripped more water on the rock of her left-rein issues, and re-experienced some of the feelings that had become a bit woolly in her own practice. In contrast, the riders in the

**Photo 8.10**
Karin and Astro look really good in trot to the left, and we see Karin in profile, with her hands level.

**Photo 8.11**
Canter left is also improving, although Karin's reins are too long and her lower leg is held against the horse's side. Astro's reach into the rein is impressive when you consider that his starting point was the push back of Photo 8.4.

previous chapters either broke new ground in their learning, or returned to ground they had not experienced for a while. But Karin's lesson simply clocked up more repetitions of patterns she has been grappling with for some time, and clarified them for her. When riders come on clinics, they hopefully go home with some new feels that they then have to work on alone; but when they have more regular lessons some of that practice is supervised. This means that there is someone there to catch them when they lose the recipe, as happens when corrections are either over-done or allowed to fade into oblivion.

When I do large public lecture–demonstrations, one of my favourite themes is talking to the audience about the idea that every breakthrough needs to be re-experienced ten thousand times before the new pattern becomes ingrained in the nervous system as the new norm. Then I ask them, 'Does that sound like purgatory?'. Invariably, they nod, mutter and even yell their assent – and few of my interactions with them yield such an intense response! Their reaction always interests me, because for me, the opposite is true. *Purgatory is always doing what you always did and always getting what you always got*, along with the same frustrations and limitations. To feel that the horse is capitalising on your weaknesses (if not actually running circles around you) is not fun. When I have something I can do that makes a difference, I find it immensely satisfying to make those repetitions, even if they are elusive, difficult, and demanding at first. If I feel that I am gaining influence, and asking the horse questions that – judging by his answers – make much more sense in his language, then I am more than happy, even if it means feeling weird, and engaging muscles I did not know I had. Mindlessly riding round and round has nothing on this, and playing the 'got it/lost it' game with your horse soon evolves into a journey that is not just half the fun, it is all that there is. Most people wish that riding were far less challenging, and that riding skills were much simpler and more easily learned; but each of those repetitions is the gift that riding offers, as you transcend old limits, build new co-ordinations, and grapple with those flaws.

# CHAPTER 9

# Focused concentration | Page

I have KNOWN PAGE FOR OVER FIFTEEN YEARS, and first met her when her charming husband brought her to England, happy for her to attend one of my courses as part of their honeymoon. At that time she had rather low tone, and my strongest memories of that course concern her obvious delight in riding, and her invention of the word 'flobby', which perfectly described the state of her body. This has been part of my vocabulary ever since, although it is a word I use with caution!

Page is a dressage judge, and she can be cajoled into teaching. But, after riding, her first love is breeding, and before she moved to Florida she owned a farm in Kansas where she bred and trained horses. During the first few years that I knew her she both hosted clinics at her farm, and travelled to California to attend further clinics. But despite her enthusiasm, I felt that my input was less effective than it should have been. It took me a while to realise that I was in competition with a number of other trainers. Kansas is (or was) the backwoods of dressage riding, so Page felt that she should take lessons with every clinician who came into town. I am quite sure that even if I left her bearing down, staying vertical and riding well, the best case scenario was that she maintained this only for as long as it took for someone else to breeze in and say something different!

'Clinic hopping' is more of an American affliction than a British one, and it can send people hither and thither. But at the other end of the spectrum, I have also seen riders show tremendous loyalty to a trainer who appears to be teaching them nothing. It can be hard to know how to advise people, but most of the riders I teach find, over time, that they become more discerning about who they ride with. Also, they learn to take input from a conventional trainer and process it through their 'Ride With Your Mind' knowledge. They translate, as if between different languages, and can have the best of both worlds without going off course.

This has taken Page longer than it takes many people, primarily because of her lack of trust in herself. She has always tended to believe an outsider in preference to herself, and to dismiss her own knowledge. (Here I find myself wishing that she had taught more, because there is nothing quite like the experience of diagnosing problems and seeing the solutions work in other people. It makes you know and understand the issues on a deeper level.) Even when Page has had a seminal new feeling, and has felt her horse change in response to the change in her body, she has easily sold out on the 'knowing it in your bones' that I want this experience to engender.

I discussed this with her recently, during a clinic that took place eight months after the one where these photographs were taken. 'I think there have been so many times when I thought I had got it, and then discovered I hadn't... so I've learned that I cannot trust myself,' she said, rather mournfully. To help make up for this she has a wonderful set of mirrors (that you see in the lesson with Carol), and she rides under supervision much more than most of the people I teach. This means that she cannot go far off course before somebody catches her. This is a huge advantage, and I know many more people who do not get *enough* feedback from an outside eye. In an ideal world this should happen at least every four weeks, giving the rider enough time to make mistakes and learn from them, but not enough time to stray too far from the straight and narrow.

While I want to encourage Page to be more self-reliant and to believe in herself more, I also know that there are huge dangers in thinking that you have 'got it'. This is rather like trying to catch running water and put it in a bucket – the moment you do that, it is not running water any more. Just as you cannot step into the same river twice, so you cannot ride the same circle twice, and every moment presents a new opportunity for interacting with your horse. If you decide that you have already 'got it' you may be tempted to absent yourself from that interaction. But whenever you stop playing the 'got it/lost it' game with your horse you are no longer riding him (in the way I understand the term), and you invite him to absent himself too. Then, when he becomes more resistant, you may well not realise that you were the one who initially 'lost it'.

I have no doubt that whenever Page thought 'I've got it!', she was indeed experiencing an important 'it', which (like every other 'it') needed to go through its ten thousand repetitions before it could become ingrained in her nervous system as the new norm. However, during the course of this it is all too easy to change the recipe, as it were, by focusing on 'flour' and forgetting that there also have to be 'eggs'. The proportions of the ingredients that are needed to bake a good 'trot cake' can easily become distorted, and we all tend to lose the overview that keeps the cake turning out just right. Knowing this, I like to warn people that 'As soon as you become addicted to the solution to your problem, that solution is likely to become your next problem' (and personally, I think this explains much of life and the whole of politics!).

There is another complication too. For as you begin to make those repetitions, the feeling will tend to become less intense. This is natural, because the nervous system habituates to it – just as you cease to notice the smell that you have been in for a while. To make the feeling just as intense as time goes by you have to do it *more*, and at some stage you will reach 'overkill'. This happens to more determined and ardent riders, who then reappear on one of my courses, and feel devastated when they have to do the exact opposite of what I was telling them last time! Mirrors, a video camera, a good friend or a good teacher could have saved them; but they had all sailed gaily on with no feedback. In fact, I once met someone who had dutifully practised the feeling from a lesson for *eight years* before she found her way back to me. Needless to say, the solution to her original problem had become her new problem!

The majority of riders are less assiduous than this, and they find that they cannot recreate the feeling, or that it fades over time. In particular, the day after the day you did it really well is always a challenge, and if you get on your horse thinking 'Right then, where's my cake?' you are bound to be disappointed (if not deeply upset and close to suicidal), because cake will not be delivered to you on a silver platter. You have to start from scratch and bake it all over again, going through every stage with equal attention and tenacity. And there is always the danger that you *think* you know the recipe, but as it fails to work, you belatedly realise that there must be more ingredients that you had not originally noticed. Or perhaps you just rode along on the previous day, thrilled that you had 'got it', and without even thinking about what you would have to do in your body to reproduce the feeling. So then it is back to the mixing bowl for some more exploration.

Not many people have the dedication and finely tuned attention that it takes to monitor each ride so closely, but this level of focus is the hallmark of skilled riders. The rub is this: as a feeling becomes less intense over time, you have to discover if it is becoming less intense because you are habituating to it, or because you are selling out on it and not really doing it. This so often happens as we become a bit lazy, or get sidetracked by something else. The question is best answered by your horse – once you are astute enough to decode his feedback. But whenever Page lost her ability to recreate 'trot cake' she decided that she must have been wrong in thinking that she had ever had it – that she had fooled herself and could not be trusted. On the contrary, she *did* have it, and had genuinely experienced a breakthrough that extended the limits of her skill at that time. But she distorted the recipe as she made those repetitions. The sad truth is that none of us is immune. I have seen even top-class riders lose the recipe.

The work I have done with Page over time has focused as much on her mental state as on her physical skills. She had to learn to concentrate, and we had a tremendous breakthrough about three years ago when I defined for her three states that I saw her operate from. One I called *'cruise control'* – she just putzed along not really paying attention, 'spacing out' and hoping things would turn out well. When they did not, she would 'come to' and resort to *'undifferentiated effort'*, in which she rode her horses 'on the muscle'. In this state she tended to resort to kick and pull, and to assume that more of what she was already doing must surely be the answer. This is the riding equivalent of shouting louder at the natives. She would even grit her teeth in determination – and

**Photo 9.1**
Sitting trot on the right rein makes a very pleasing picture. Page can match the forces which the horse's movement exerts on her body.

her horses probably gritted their teeth too! After that, she often *threw in the towel*. As an opera singer in her youth, she is no stranger to the theatrical. 'That's it,' I have heard her say, 'I'll never ride this horse! He's so sensitive, and I'm such a klutz. He just won't **!!!**.... I just can't ****!!!*... and my left hand is a CRIMINAL! It should be CHOPPED OFF!'

The fourth possibility we called '*noticing mode*', and finding this has changed Page's riding more than anything else. In noticing mode she monitors her body and her horse's body, riding on interface from moment to moment. If she catches things before they go very far wrong, she is less tempted to resort to brute force and ignorance as she attempts to make them right. She makes smaller corrections more frequently. She does not get 'wound up', and does not 'throw in the towel'. She simply notices, and reads her horse, responding to his

**Photo 9.2**
In canter right Promeso's neck looks more 'scrunched', with a more closed 'V' shape under his gullet, and less of a curve to his crest.

142

contortions with the best corrections her body can muster.

As a strategy for riding and learning this works far better than allowing yourself to 'space out'. It also works better than simply trying to be obedient. A little obedience helps us to get the learning process rolling, and if it is all you can do at your existing skill level, so be it. It will get you started. But sooner or later you have to *transcend* obedience and learn to improvise as you respond to your horse. Obedience will get you into trouble, because the formula you are applying will soon become outdated.

Over the years, I have taught Page on a variety of mostly home-bred horses who have been sold when the need to run a real business collided hard enough with her love for them. ('I cried all the way to the bank,' she told me once, 'but my husband was so proud of me!') The horse that Page rode in this clinic is Promeso, a nine-year-old Andalusian, bred by a friend of hers. He was an orphan foal, and as a six-year-old he had still not been backed, so Page took him on. **Photo 9.1** shows sitting trot on the right rein, and they both present a pleasing picture. Page's alignment is good, although her head is forward of the ideal. But more important than this, she, like Heather, can match the forces that the horse's movement exerts on her body. If they were sitting on a 'space hopper' ball (popular with kids some years ago), Page and Heather would be proactively making it bounce forward; but most riders would topple off the back of it as it bounced away from them.

**Photo 9.2** shows Promeso in canter on the right rein, and here it would be better if he had a more open 'U' shape under his gullet. This would make the underside of his neck into a softer curve. But if you compare **Photos 9.1** and **9.2** with **Photo 9.3**, which shows left rein trot, you see how much tighter this can become, with the underside of his neck almost vertical and a very tight 'V' under his gullet. In **Photo 9.1** his crest makes an even curve from wither to poll, while in **Photo 9.3** it looks, to quote trainer Charles de Kunffy, 'as if he has been sword swallowing'. It extends out of the wither in a straight line, but then it suddenly changes angle in front of the third vertebra. This is the highest point of his neck, which dips down from here to make his poll lower. Promeso is looking to the left, but he only does so from this point where his neck 'breaks'. Page's body still looks well lined up, but the photograph also shows her left hand behind her right – showing us why she might regard it as a criminal!

Many riders are thrilled when their horse's nose is vertical, and this is their sole aim. So they do not notice the tight 'V' shape under the gullet, and/or the lack of a curve in the crest. They also do not notice if the horse's nose is behind the vertical, and many horses (whether or not they are overbent) look as if they have a huge head rammed into the end of a scrawny neck. Their riders seem not to realise *how non-beautiful and non-classical this is* – perhaps they think that they were just unfortunate to buy a horse who was born in this shape. What they have not appreciated is the power of more or less skilled riding to create the shapes of **Photos 9.1** and **9.3**. They also have not yet discovered how changing the shape of a horse's back changes how he moves, and changes the shape of his whole body. (Remember the exercise (**Fig. 4.1**) on page 69 in Chapter 4 (Jo) where you walked as if you were a horse, and experienced the difference between your back being rounded or dropped.) In **Photos 9.1** and **9.3** we could be comparing a horse that is 'through' with one that is not. But realise that we are looking at *both sides of the same horse*, and we are seeing a pattern that has, over recent years, typified Page's riding, and the 'stamp' she has put on her horses. Although she looks much more aligned than Sue or Karin, her right and left sides could well belong to two different people.

Working with a rider over a long period of time allows us to track her asymmetry through the layers of the onion, peeling it away so that we can home in on its root causes. Initially Page's biggest problem seemed to be on the right rein, for in that direction she came off axis, with her torso curving to the right and creases in the right side of her waistband. Page's pattern is to press into the right stirrup and to lift her right seat bone as she makes those creases. This means that she does the *opposite* of Sue and Karin, who make their creases on the side of the seat bone that gets heavier. It took me a while to diagnose Page's issues accurately, for I used to assume that the creases would always be on the side of the heavier seat bone. While this is by far the most common pattern, it is not always the case.

In our early asymmetry lessons, Page had to lighten her right foot, lift her right knee, and think of her right thigh much more out in front of her, for every time she pushed down into the stirrup it became too vertical. Adding the boards exercise increased her ability to straighten her torso and keep her chin over the horse's mane. However, it revealed that while the right board was weak and had creases in it (which led to the obvious creases in her torso), her left board was nowhere to be found. Her left side was floating off the left side of the horse, and discovering this made her realise that her issues with straightness involved more than just her right side.

Every asymmetry issue must, by definition, involve both sides of the body. For if one side is creased, then the other must be stretched, and if one is rotated back the other is rotated forward. Riders often try to fix an asymmetry problem *as if it only exists on one side*, but the truth is that both reins and both sides must have their issues. However, these are different and complementary issues, which form opposite sides of the same coin.

Thus I have realised over the years that behind every overt problem lies a covert problem, which holds the obvious problem in place. Usually it is on the other side of the body, and I distinctly remember the lesson in which Page discovered the covert problem with her left side, realising its contribution to the problem that she had thought lay only in her right side. I remember her muttering, 'Oh my goodness. It's the left side … the left side … but I always thought the problem was on the right.' Involving the left side helped her to find a better fix for the overt problem on the right side, and eventually the fixes on the right became so good that her left side and the left rein became the most significant issue – for most of the time, at least.

Whenever you make a significant improvement in the 'bad' side and bad rein it never just catches up with the 'good' rein, as most people hope and expect. Instead it becomes better than the good rein… so the rider's great reward for her efforts is a new 'bad' rein! Like Page, most people experience a significant shock when they first discover the covert problems in the 'good' side – and when it later becomes the 'bad' side they are often horrified! But this evolution (which may happen many times) peels away yet another layer of the onion. As long as the rider can move the problem down a layer, and not just ping-pong between two options, she is making progress. In working with asymmetries, the rider's greatest need is to develop the 'brain space' which enables her to think about both sides of her body in quick succession, if not both at the same time. This is a form of mental dexterity that eludes most people for quite some time, but I guarantee that if you ride along thinking 'right, right, right, right, right', then it is only a matter of time before you wake up with a problem on the left. Yet again, your attempt to solve your problem will have become your next problem.

In *For the Good of the Rider* I drew an analogy between learning to ride, and sailing in a boat that has leaks in it. Firstly there is the obvious question of whether you should be sailing or bailing, and how you can possibly manage both at the same time! Bailing is like taking time to focus primarily on your riding skills, hopefully to the point where you start fixing those leaks. Sailing without bailing is like ignoring problems that actually stop you from sailing your boat (or training your horse). But realise too that once you have managed to fix the most obvious leak, you might get a few minutes' or a few days' grace before the next biggest leak reveals itself as a problem. Fix that, and the next biggest leak will become your new problem … and so it goes on.

At each stage a leak that might once have seemed insignificant becomes the issue that hampers your progress. Even though those leaks are actually much smaller issues than the ones you have solved previously, they will seem just as large, and – human nature being what it is – they will annoy you just as much! You might even contrive not to realise that you are improving, for you are always facing a problem. Alternatively, you might kid yourself that after you have solved this problem then surely you will have 'arrived'. But all that ever happens is that the problem moves on. Your perceptions are becoming more refined, your body control is becoming more refined, and you are playing the 'got it/lost it' game with your horse on an increasingly sophisticated level. You cannot 'arrive' because if your backside is in the saddle, the game does not stop. Your horse has no 'off' switch (even though he might sometimes like to kid you that he has).

I rode Promeso on one of the days that I was staying with Page, and this really helped me to diagnose how they interacted with each other. I like to think of the horse and rider fitting together like two pieces of a jigsaw puzzle, and Promeso duly took up his habitual jigsaw shape and expected me to fit around him like Page. But I realised how differently he was organising his two sides, and attempted not to fall into the expected pattern. On the contrary, I wanted to repattern him by making a more correct jigsaw-puzzle shape with my own left side, giving him a new shape to fit around.

Horses can make this more or less easy for the rider to do, and I am never sure if it is the good news or the bad news when a more skilled rider gets on your horse and announces: 'This is really easy' – meaning that your lack of skill is the most significant problem; or 'His pattern is really difficult to change' – meaning that your horse is setting you a problem that even a professional finds challenging! Promeso's pattern fell somewhere in between these extremes. If he were a stuffed-toy horse his right side would have been very well stuffed, but his left side would have been very unstuffed. This is not unusual; but he had a particularly clever way of using his left side to *drag the stuffing out of me*.

Teachers of Tai Chi, talk about the 'full side' and the 'empty side', and this describes very well what can happen to riders and horses. The 'full' side of the body has much higher tone than the other side, and very few people are evenly toned or stuffed either from side to side or from top to bottom. Part of Heather's talent lies in the evenness of her tone. Page's right side is much more highly toned than her left, and bizarre as this sounds, it functions as if it were a vacuum cleaner, which can vacuum the horse's inner contents into his back and into Page's body, keeping them 'full'. But on the left side, Promeso vacuums the inner contents of both of them into his left shoulder, left foreleg, and the left side of his mouth. These may be 'full', but his back is 'empty'. So is the left side of Page's torso – and with the power and stuffing leached out of it, she cannot even really sense it. Her left hand and arm, however, are full, and pitted against the fullness of Promeso's forehand. Hence their criminal tendencies.

As you sit in your chair, imagine suctioning strength into one side of your body, and letting the strength leach out of the other side. Then reverse sides, realise how strange this feels, and diagnose where you too would lose strength.

**Photo 9.4**
Page's left side is far weaker than her right. To strengthen the muscles in the left side of her front and to make it possible for her to push her left hand forward, I am giving her a resistance to push that hand against.

You might be amazed at how obvious this is, and since we are talking here not just about your muscle tone but also about your 'energy body', the exercise gives you an insight into the 'energetics' of riding.

Page knew about the criminal behaviour of her left hand, and she berated and hated herself for it. But her attempts to tame it were doomed, for it was merely a symptom. Meanwhile, she had been completely unaware of how the left side of her torso was being constantly 'emptied' by her horse's little trick. This was so much a part of the *status quo* of their interaction that she had become like the goldfish who would not discover water. All she could tell me was that her left side always felt nebulous, and that all her attempts to make it feel more stuffed, more strong, and more 'there' (to her feel sense) had failed.

In cases like this, one is often left wondering who is the chicken and who is the egg. Did Page's jigsaw-puzzle shape encourage Promeso to organise himself like this, or did his shape disorganise her into doing this? In this case, I fear that it is the former, for I also rode one of Page's four-year-olds, who gave me more than an inkling of the same feeling. Our work on changing the pattern began with the exercise in **Photo 9.4**, where I am giving Page a resistance to push her left hand against. I wanted her to push it forward instead of pulling it back – but more importantly, I also wanted her to bear down more in the left side of her front, and to feel how the muscles could become a stronger wall. I wanted her to do a left-handed version of the exercise you did on page 45 (**Fig. 2.6**).

Page is one of those rare riders who finds it easier to organise her body when she is going laterally than when she is going straight, so we used the lateral movements to try to help her gain more clarity about what was happening. (We will talk more about the 'how' of riding them in the next chapter.) It was actually in shoulder-in left that Page first felt how Promeso started to elongate and empty his left side, thus making hers feel more nebulous. The moment of positioning him into the movement gave her a heightened sense of the need to keep his left side well inflated underneath her, and it became the moment when she felt him slip it away from her. But more importantly, she felt her own left side slip away with it. This was the 'Aha!' moment that I was hoping to generate, for, like all of us, Page *cannot change any issue in her riding while she is unaware that it is happening.*

**Photo 9.5**

This shoulder-in left, in trot, is just on four tracks. Page is well aligned, with her zipper vertical and over Promeso's mane. Although Page is controlling his shoulders well the right side of his neck does not look very stuffed.

**Photo 9.6**

As we look at shoulder-in left from behind we see Page's and Promeso's left sides. Page is still vertical, with her shoulders level and horizontal creases in her waistcoat. The muscles on the left side of Promeso's neck are bulging more than one might expect and more than the muscles of his right side in Photo 8.5. This is because they contain the stuffing that he has dragged forward out of his ribcage.

You can see in **Photos 9.5** and **9.6** that what resulted was a fairly good shoulder-in. Page looks very straight – her chin is over the horse's mane, and the creases in her waistcoat are even on both sides. Her torso really does look box-shaped, with no distortions. The shoulder-in is just on four tracks, so we can see each of Promeso's feet. (If it were on three tracks, the inside hind would be lined up with and hidden by the outside fore.) **Photo 9.5** shows a good bend to the left, but **Photo 9.6**, where we see the muscles of the left side of his neck, shows that they still do not form the ideal curves from the wither to the poll, and from the wither to the left.

On the right rein, I asked Page to ride renvers, which is a less well-known movement. As you see in **Photo 9.7** renvers keeps the horse's legs in the same position as shoulder-in, but asks him to bend towards the way he is going. This meant that Promeso's left side was the inside (not the outside). With that side of the horse shorter it became easier for Page to organise herself, and not let either Promeso's left side or her own left side slip away from her. This is the advantage of renvers, and many riders find it easier than shoulder-in (although most trainers will tell you that it is harder). Page may be leaning slightly to the right, but she was beginning to build well on that 'Aha!' moment.

Encouraged by her successes, Page made several attempts at half-pass. This movement more than any other tends to distort the rider's torso, and as you see in **Photo 9.8** she has regressed to her original problem, which in most situations she has solved. Her torso is curving to the right – for in a rather desperate attempt to make the movement happen she has pushed into her right stirrup (with her toe, not her heel), and has lifted her right seat bone. We did not pursue this in the lesson, as I did not want to confuse her. But she would

**Photo 9.7**
Page rides renvers on the left rein. This keeps Promeso's legs in the same position as they are in shoulder-in left, but it reverses the bend. So his left side is now both in the direction of motion and on the inside of the curve in his body. This makes it easier for Page to organise Promeso's left side. If it were on the outside of the curve he could 'run his number' more easily.

**Photo 9.8**
Page rides half-pass left, but in her attempt to make the movement happen she has reverted to her original asymmetry problem. She has pushed into her right stirrup, lifted her right seat bone, and leant to the right, distorting the 'box' of her torso.

probably have needed to come back to walk to reduce the size of the forces acting on her body, and to give her more time and more 'brain space' for making the correction.

Page gradually realised that, whether she was going straight or laterally, she had to keep the left side of her front as a really strong wall, which stopped Promeso from being able to 'suck' the strength out of her. Instead of acting like

**Photo 9.9**
In trot to the left Promeso looks better than he did, but his neck still shows that the same pattern is operating, albeit to a lesser extent.

**Photo 9.10**
This photo was taken eight months later, and after more practice in stopping Promeso from making her 'leaky' Page has become able to suction stuffing and power into both of their left sides. Compare the shape of his neck with Photo 9.3. Very few riders are ever able to change a horse's carriage like this – it requires tools that go beyond the conventional wordscape!

a permeable membrane it had to act like a dam that enabled her insides to contain the pressure of much more stuffing. She also had to be careful to stop her left seat bone from being pulled forward as Promeso elongated his left side. She had to keep her underneath down on the saddle, thinking of it as a long flat surface that he could not scrunch up. (Remember how this helped Diane.) Thus she was able to stop him from distorting the bottom of her box-shaped torso.

The improvement we generated led to the trot of **Photo 9.9**, which was better but not fantastic. There was much more improvement in the clinic eight months later, when Page was able to take the next step – she had had a lot of practice in stopping Promeso from making her 'leaky', and she was then able to become more proactive, and to use her left side to generate suction. This made both her left side and his left operate far more like their right sides, as you see in **Photo 9.10**. Notice how Promeso's crest is a far more even curve than it is in **Photos 9.2** and **9.3**. The muscles in her left thigh and left side really began to ache, making her realise the degree to which they had not been working. But she was greatly relieved to discover that her left hand was far more able to give forward!

By the time I see her next, no doubt the game that she plays with her horse will have moved on. I hope to find that she has peeled away another layer of the onion, improved her 'bumprint', and become more discerning. If she can stay in 'noticing mode' this is almost inevitable, for concentration is the name of the game. Truly, it is the Master art.

# CHAPTER 10

# Lateral work | Denise

I have KNOWN DENISE FOR EVEN LONGER than I have known Page, and have watched with great satisfaction as her life has been transformed by the skills she has learned in the riding arena. Until five years ago she was a senior nurse, working in theatre and recovery – and her stamina was constantly tested by the need to care for and ride her horses alongside her working hours. As her riding skills evolved so did her desire to change her life style and to pass on her knowledge. She now combines teaching riding with saddle fitting, and is one of the senior coaches of my work.

Over the years I have taught her on a number of horses, but the light of her life is undoubtedly Piper, now nineteen, who is of unknown Irish breeding. He was bought at nine as her husband's hunter, but four years later Denise borrowed him to ride a Preliminary dressage test. Her long-suffering husband lost his horse – and Piper began a training that has taken him to Advanced Medium (Third) level. During those years a couple of complex health issues have laid his career on the line, but despite these he has become a shining ball of muscle, who can do more than a few steps of piaffe and passage, as well as flying changes. He is an absolute tribute to Denise's nursing and management, and also to the riding skills she has developed through her tenacity as a pupil.

Nothing gives me more pleasure than to see a horse who is not a 'dressage horse' outshine those who have the right breeding, but are not ridden so skilfully. Few people really appreciate that any horse – whatever his make and shape – will look like 'a dressage horse' when he comes up through his back and reaches into the rein. The biomechanics of correct movement create the outline that dressage riders crave, and conformation faults disappear in that overall picture. Long necks or big heads are no longer visible, and at the same time a horse's paces can be significantly improved. Piper will never move like a well-bred warmblood, but he has delighted Denise both with his exceptional

**Photo 10.1**
Denise warms Piper up in canter right, bringing his back up and reaching his neck 'deep and round' into the rein so that his nose comes behind the vertical. She looks well aligned and firmly stuffed.

aptitude for collected work, and with his ability to find the extended trot that she once despaired of.

Denise has often despaired as well about her own body, longing for long, thin legs and a sylph-like frame. Over the years she has taken lessons with a number of the dressage trainers who visit her area, and a couple have made it clear to her that their client group would not extend to include a short woman on a wide cob. Others were so disparaging that their 'lessons' were a bad investment. Denise has desperately wanted to take Piper to the upper levels of dressage, and happily, she has now found some higher-quality competition-based input. As well as working with me, she trades lessons with a successful

**Photo 10.2**
In rising trot too, Denise works Piper deep and round.

competition rider who has become fascinated by the world of biomechanics.

Denise warms Piper up very carefully, using more walk and canter work than one might with a younger horse, and working him quite deep and round. **Photo 10.1** shows him in canter right, and **Photo 10.2** shows rising trot on the left rein. By **Photo 10.3** Denise has gone sitting and has brought him up into his competition frame. But before she brings his *front* up she makes sure she has brought his *back* up, and one of the most significant issues here is that she has a choice about how she positions him.

In raising Piper's forehand, Denise faces many of the same challenges that faced Diane, whose horse overbent. Diane could not combat this evasion while she was growing up tall and stretching her legs down (as in **Photo 6.1** on page 97), but notice in contrast how Denise has a much more acute angle between the front of her torso and her thigh. She has to keep her front tendons up (**Photo 4.8**, page 79 in the chapter with Jo) and 'hold up the tea tray' (**Photo 6.8**, page 108, Diane). Both riders have to think (as explained in **Fig. 6.5** on page 106) of not letting the horse arch his back so much that he curls away from under her pubic bone. Denise keeps her underneath as a long, flat surface that stays in contact with a longer, flatter surface of Piper's back. Also, her torso acts as a good carousel pole.

In fact, Denise's mechanics mirror the photos of Heather in Chapter 2. She might not be so inherently elegant as a rider, but she has 'cloned' the essence of Heather's body pattern. Her two worst mistakes are having her head forward while looking down, and also having her lower leg in front of its ideal shoulder/hip/heel alignment. In fact, she is aligned better in the rising trot and canter of **Photos 10.2** and **10.1** than she is while sitting in **Photo 10.3**; but in all of the photographs she has a very nice texture to her muscles. This has been hard won. As someone who was once 'flobby' she, like Page, has progressively developed

Photo 10.3
Denise has gone sitting, and has bought Piper's forehand up, bringing him into his competition frame. Her reins are rather long, and both her head and her lower leg are too far forward; but she is able to match the forces which the horse's movement exerts on her body.

**Photo 10.4**
As we look at Denise from behind we can see that she has a slight 'C' curve to the right, with her head tilted right, and a more closed angle on the right between her thigh and her torso.

her muscle tone through years of riding. Heather's tone has developed from a place of natural talent that made her starting point far closer to the ideal. It was always easy for Heather to match the forces which the horse's movement exerted on her body; Denise has developed this ability by 'dripping water on the rock'.

In **Photo 10.4** Denise is seen from behind in halt, and is showing us her slight tendency to make a 'C' curve to the right. Most notably, her head is to the right, and there is a more closed angle on her right side between her thigh and her torso. The pattern is similar to Sue in **Photo 7.6** (page 119), although Denise's deviation is minimal by comparison. However, it is still enough to give her a slightly heavier right seat bone, and a right lower leg that wants to come forward, as we see in **Photo 10.3**. Denise has worked long and hard on this, peeling away the layers of her asymmetry. She no longer looks rotated to the right, and she rarely comes off axis, but her right lower leg has proved the most intractable part of the pattern. This is largely because the effects of her asymmetry are coupled with the difficulty she has in extending her body control all the way down to her feet on both sides. I have often found myself reassuring Denise that there *will* be a day when her legs behave themselves, but even though they flap much less than they used to in sitting trot, she still does not believe me. The answer lies – as you might expect – in those deeper layers of the onion.

One of the biggest challenges for Denise has been the lateral movements, which have demanded more tone and more organisation than she could easily muster. The challenge of stabilising the body on the side/side plane is greater on a circle than on a straight line, but I believe it is magnified times *ten* in leg-yield and shoulder-in, and *by ten again* in half-pass. This explains why so many riders struggle. Page is extremely unusual in that these movements have often helped her to increase her tone and become more organised. Most riders – Denise included – take a very long time to reach that stage, and only as their skill increases can the movements become useful training exercises.

**Photos 10.5** and **10.6** show leg-yield in walk and trot, with the horse's tail to the wall. I find this movement more helpful for learning riders than a leg-yield with the horse parallel to the long side of the arena and moving (say) from the centre line back to the track. I often see horses wandering vaguely sideways as the rider attempts this, with her convinced that she is doing much better than she actually is. Putting the horse at an angle to the wall makes the issues much clearer, like writing them in capital letters. If the rider is struggling to position the horse I can help from the ground (as I did with Gina in the 1991 *Masterclass* book). Or I can suggest that she positions the horse's head towards the wall. With this barrier in front of him, they will both be less likely to pull on the reins.

In both photographs Piper is just on four tracks, at about a 30° angle to the wall. Both horse and rider look very straight, and there is no bend in Piper's body as there would be in shoulder-in. Denise's shoulders are level, and as she comes towards us we see her zipper stacked up directly over Piper's mane. As she goes away from us, we see that the creases in her waistcoat look level and even. This is no mean feat, and the first challenge of leg-yield is to bring the horse's shoulders away from the wall without pulling on the inside rein and without any deviations in your torso. The former is everyone's first instinct, but it will only succeed in bringing the horse's *neck* to the inside, while his shoulders remain by the wall – which means that his response is to jack-knife, just as he would on a circle. As the rider's inside hand pulls back, her outside hand gives forward, and often, her torso rotates with her hands. The advancing of her outside shoulder and outside hand effectively gives the horse a gap for his outside shoulder to fall through. The more desperate the rider becomes, the more likely she is to increase the size of that gap, turning her shoulders too much and leaning to the inside.

By this time, she may have no weight at all on her outside seat bone. Ideally she would be keeping them evenly weighted and moving them appropriately with the horse's gait, controlling the speed of their movement so that she controls the speed of his legs. She would also be bearing down, breathing well, and giving her hand forward. But more often she sucks her stomach in, grows tall, pulls on the reins, and stops breathing. As she pulls back she will probably open the 'A' frame of her thighs so wide that they can do nothing to help her position the horse's wither. Then, all she is left with is the reins. In her desperation to make the movement happen she has become her own (and the horse's) worst enemy. She may seize up so completely that her seat bones stop moving – and so does her horse. Or she may start shoving at him with her inside seat bone, as

10.5

10.6

**Photo 10.5**
Leg-yield in walk on the left rein. Piper's body is straight and he is on four tracks. Thus we see each of his feet. Denise has her zipper vertical and her shoulders horizontal.

**Photo 10.6**
Denise is now leg-yielding in trot, and as we look at her from behind we can see that she is stacked up vertically, with level shoulders and horizontal creases in her waistcoat.

she attempts to move him away from it. All of these tactics are highly instinctive, but the more the rider weights that seat bone and leans away from the direction of motion, the more the horse refuses to budge. This is by far the most likely option, but the more reactive 'wizzy' horse may enact the sideways version of waterski/motorboat, and run away with her in that jack-knife!

None of these options make a pretty picture, or a helpful aid to training. Many authors extol the training benefits of leg-yield and shoulder-in, as if they are movements sent from heaven. At a certain skill level this is true, but personally, I think they are sent by the devil to tempt you – all over again – to pull, kick, and shove. Just when you thought you had learned to bear down, keep yourself aligned, lift the horse's back and ride him 'from back to front', so, on this deeper layer of the onion, you are again faced with the temptation to 'end gain' (i.e. to get the end result without paying attention to the means whereby). So you make the movement happen somehow – *anyhow*. When faced with the demands of the lateral movements, you are an unusually talented rider if you do not have *to learn those correct baselines all over again*.

When I was a young rider, my teachers taught shoulder-in by telling me to position my horse as if I were about to ride a circle, and then, when his forehand had come one step away from the track, I was to 'change my mind' and ride him along the wall instead. But I could never make this work, because nobody told me that along with changing my mind I also had to change the position of my seat bones. So I changed my mind with my hands, contorted myself in the ways described above, and my early attempts – like Denise's – were based on push/pull. If only our teachers could have put their 'know-how' into words, explaining just how the rider/horse interaction works when his steps go sideways! It takes more than explanations, however, for withstanding those forces requires the correct kind of strength that stops the 'box' of the torso from deforming, both in the face of those forces, and also in the face of instincts that tempt us into those self-defeating contortions.

I like to explain the basic idea to riders by putting a stick on the ground, and suggesting that it represents the midline of the horse's spine and crest (**Fig. 10.1**). I then place my fists on each side of it, as if they represented the rider's seat bones. On a circle these are in the ten to four positioning on the left rein, and the ten past eight positioning on the right rein (as explained on page 133, Karin). Imagine that our 'horse' is on a circle, but that we want to position him into a lateral movement in which his quarters are on a smaller circle than his shoulders. The fists/seat bones can move his central axis into this position by coming into a more exaggerated position themselves – the outside seat bone moves back to give us the positioning of five to five on the left rein, and five past seven on the right.

Then suppose that we want instead to position the horse/stick so that he moves laterally with his shoulders on a smaller circle than his quarters. We then have to reverse the positioning of the fists/seat bones. The advancing outside seat bone brings the horse's shoulders to the inside, giving us the five past seven

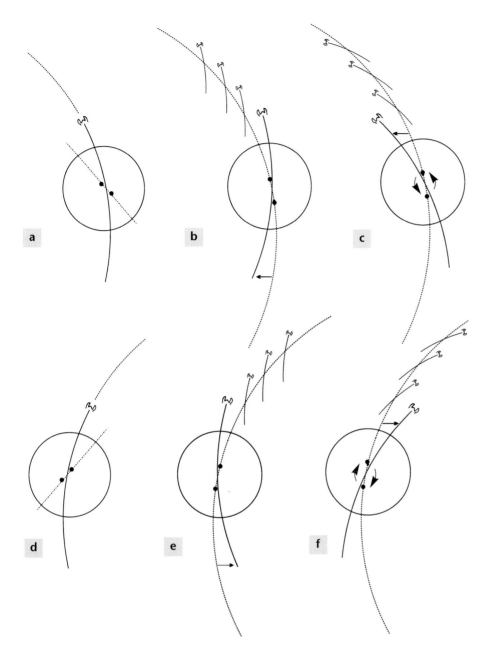

Fig. 10.1
How the rider's seat bones can be used to position the horse's central axis (and your fists can be used to position a stick that is lying on the ground).

In (a), (b) and (c) the horse is on the left rein. In (d), (e) and (f) he is on the right rein.

(a) and (d) show the basic circle positioning, with the seat bones/fists at ten to four on the left rein, and ten past eight on the right rein.

(b) and (e) show how making those positions more extreme brings the horse's quarters in on a circle. This gives us the five to five position on the left rein, and the five past seven position on the right. The horse/stick can then be moved sideways on the circle in travers.

(c) and (f) show how reversing the position of the seat bones brings the horse's forehand in on the circle. This gives us the five past seven position on the left rein and the five to five position on the right rein. The horse/stick can then be moved sideways on the circle in shoulder-in.

positioning on the left rein and the five to five positioning on the right. This explanation has helped many people to understand how to position the horse for the lateral movements, and I recommend that you find a long stick and do it. It has an impeccable logic; but if it sends your brain into a spin, just realise that the challenge is to position him and you so that there are no deformations in either his longitudinal axis or your vertical axis.

Thus Denise's success with Piper is based on the way she has turned the whole of him and the whole of her, while keeping her spine vertical and the front of her torso at a right angle to his crest. So she is no longer in the fencing-lunge position of the circle, with her outside seat bone back. As she asks for the leg-yield she advances it, making sure that it keeps bearing its fifty per cent share of her weight. Her outside aids must continue to make a good wall, just as they do on a circle. The change in seat bone position is critical; but Denise has evolved beyond the point of just thinking about this. She has also positioned the horse's wither with her thighs, keeping them snugly in place so that he is contained by her 'A' frame. There is no 'wriggle room' between her thighs, which he might use to 'wriggle' his withers back towards the track. He is also held in place by her boards, which are both on, and by her outer thirds which are still stuffed and stacked, keeping her epaulets aligned over each of his long back muscles. When she hits it just right, her hands have virtually nothing to do. As she continues up the long side she will probably have to keep adjusting herself into this position, and as long as she succeeds in this there is very little that her horse can do about it – even if leg-yield is not his favourite option!

Think of the muscle chains that pass from the horse's croup to his poll, on each side of his spine, like a pair of skis. Good training does indeed make those muscle chains act like skis, but initially they are highly unlikely to be a matching pair. In Promeso, the knock-on effects of this were visible in the shape of his neck on each side, as shown in **Photos 9.1** and **9.3**, pages 142 and 143. The skis might have different widths, and be at different heights. One or both of them might be soggy, wiggly, broken into several pieces, or tilted with the outer edge down. The horse's contribution to steering issues of all descriptions will lie in his dysfunctional skis, and in the way he holds his ribcage beneath them – for it will be displaced to the side of the stronger ski, holding it up. Meanwhile, the soggy, narrow, or tilted ski has no firm base to rest on.

Once the rider can position her seat bones, steer the horse's wither, and get both boards on, she starts to influence those skis and make them more of a pair. She starts to *feel* them as they lie under the panels of the saddle, and to realise just how the horse is contorting them. She does her utmost to position her seat bones on their inside edges, without any of the wiggling or shoving that would disconnect them – so she remains 'plugged in' to those skis. She then does her best to stack her outer thirds up over their width, all the way from the neck of the femur at the bottom to the epaulets at the top. (**Fig. 10.2**, but see also **Fig. 8.4b**, page 134) But until she learns to get 'both boards on', one of her seat bones and thirds will inevitably lie too far from the horse's midline, falling off that long back muscle. She might ride that way for a lifetime, or might 'ping-

**Fig. 10.2**
Drawing (a) shows how the rider's seat bones should ideally lie on the inner edges of the horse's long back muscles (the outer edges of the gullet of the saddle). The neck of the femur then lies across the horse's long back muscle (the ski) with the trochanter of the femur lying on the outer edge of the muscle. However, most riders have 'one side on and one side off', and in (b) the seat bone on the right side of the page is too far away from the horse's midline, so that the neck of the femur and the trochanter are falling off the edge of the muscle. The rider will struggle to ride this side of the horse.

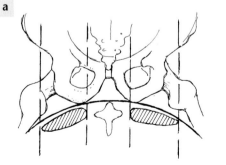
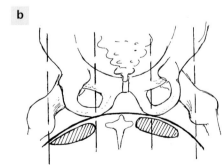

pong' from time to time as the side that is on trades places with the side that is off. As we discussed earlier, this means that she will have a 'good rein' and a 'bad rein' that sometimes trade places.

The more the rider becomes able to stuff and stack her outer thirds, the more she becomes able to influence the width, height, and levelness of the horse's long back muscles, making them fit into the distance between her seat bones and the greater trochanter of the femur. Karin, Page and Denise are working on this – but it is not so easy, particularly as the horse will tend to mirror the rider. So if she has a soggy, unstuffed side, the horse will be unstuffed under her. If one of her outer thirds lacks width, so too will the ski underneath it. This makes the fix doubly difficult, and it means that *the rider's fundamental challenge is to work on herself*. If she contorts herself to steer, she becomes an even bigger part of the problem, exacerbating the pre-existing contortions in the skis. Then she will struggle like Sue. In fact, the horse and rider reflect each other in ways that make us question – as we did with Page – just who is the chicken and who is the egg.

Realise that when the rider is on a circle, the skis do not actually bend, as so many people assume. But neither do they bend in skiing. As the horse 'turns like a bus', the skis keep equal width and height, and the rider might (or might not) choose to flex their tips to the inside. In shoulder-in, travers, renvers and half-pass, the front parts of the skis curve more than they do at any other time, but the skis under the saddle must stay wide and level. In lateral movements, the horse's legs cross, but the skis/muscle chains do not. The rider begins the movement by changing the direction in which the skis are facing (e.g. from parallel to the long side of the arena to that 30° angle that Denise is showing us). Even in a leg-yield, they ideally make that change from the back forward, rather than pivoting about the middle, as intimated by our analogy above. This is its limitation; but as the rider's skills increase (and as she also learns to ride a turn on the haunches, which I shall not discuss here) so she can affect this change from further back on the horse.

So imagine that riding a lateral movement is like side-stepping on skis. We will imagine them as well-formed skis, not the narrow, soggy or broken ones that have not yet been influenced by skilled riding (and when it comes to the lateral movements, fools rush in where angels fear to tread!). As you side-stepped, each ski would be moved over in its turn. But if you were side-stepping *down the side of a mountain* you would have to be very careful not to let your leading ski slide away from you, or you might do the splits! Your muscles would have to be just as concerned about limiting the movement of that ski and keeping you stacked up over it as they would with making its step happen. If you leant towards the uphill side of the mountain you would make your plight even worse, as both skis would now slide out from under you. So you have to be extremely careful how you step. Now imagine that your legs have been amputated, and that it is your seat bones and the necks of the femur that are strapped to the skis. You still side-step, and you must not let either the downhill ski, or both skis, slide away from you.

I think this image wonderfully describes the challenges of a lateral step, which inherently replicates that slippery mountainside. The seat bone and/or the ski in the direction of motion will tend to slip away from you, so when your normally lighter seat bone is on that side you will struggle to keep it 'plugged in'. Lose the seat bone and it is virtually impossible to influence that ski! The horse's long back muscle on the side in the direction of motion is highly likely to distort, and the more desperate you become, and the more you start to lean and shove with the other seat bone, the more you lose the one in the direction of motion.

The vast majority of riders over-use the side of the body they are moving the horse away from, and under-use the side they are moving towards. This is like leaning up the mountain and losing both skis down the mountain. It is our instinctive response to the challenge of a lateral step, as if we expect our horses to slide out from under us just like those skis. Naïvely we assume that this would be a success! But in contrast, most horses refuse to move. Just ask yourself how your instincts would operate if you were carrying a child on your back who kept putting her weight to one side: would you stay under her weight or move away from her weight? This analogy may help you realise that the horse who slides out from under you like those skis, and runs away with you in a jack-knife, is making a very *kamikaze* gesture! It is the sane horse who refuses to move!

Thus the key to riding the lateral movements well lies in *keeping up with the horse*, for as soon as you 'lean up the mountain' you suffer the consequences of being left behind. The third of your body in the direction of motion must remain stuffed and stacked over that side of the horse's body, controlling and containing that long back muscle. This requires a form of muscle-power that

Photos 10.7–10.8
Shoulder-in right in trot looks well organised. Piper is dead on three tracks, and Denise is stacked up all the way up to her epaulets. Notice how her whole torso is at a right angle to Piper's spine (even though her seat bones are in a more extreme position than this).

contradicts both your instincts, and the forces inherent in the movement. It is like swimming against a strong tide instead of letting the current take you. So I like to suggest that riders imagine someone standing at the far end of the long side, who has strings attached to their shoulder and waist. This person then reels them in. It as if they are being drawn towards that direction, helping them to keep up with the horse, and not over-use the side they are moving away from. For every time this seat bone moves the horse over, the other seat bone must catch him, and stay directly under a well-stacked torso – just as it would stop that ski from sliding down the mountain.

Photos **10.7** and **10.8** show Denise moving toward and away from us in trot on the right rein, now in shoulder-in. Piper does not show much bend, but he is not dead straight as he was in **Photos 10.5** and **10.6.** He is also exactly on three tracks. It is hard in shoulder-in to add a bend, but not let the horse jack-knife, and not let the outside ski slip away from you. So I also suggest that riders pay attention to the front vertical edge of the box which is in the direction of motion, and then imagine it defined by a re-bar (the steel reinforcing bars that are used in concrete pillars) that lies just inside their ribcage. This pillar must be kept firm and vertical, so that it stays stacked over the pillar of the horse's leading foreleg. It leads the way down the long side, and if the rider then thinks of filling out that front part of her ribcage (as if with more stuffing) the horse firms up and fills out under her. This is an example of the rule that wherever you need to stuff the horse's body more, you stuff yourself in the same area – in this case the leading front quadrant of both of you.

If you are still struggling to limit the horse's desire to jack-knife, the easiest way is often to ride renvers, as Page did on page 149, **Photo 9.7.** This keeps the horse's feet in the same position as shoulder-in, but it reverses the bend, putting it towards the direction of motion. So this side of the horse is kept shorter, and your seat bone/ski is less likely to slide away from the midline. Moving between the options of renvers, a straight horse (who is leg-yielding), and shoulder-in, can really help you 'nail' how your seat bones need to be, and teach you how to keep your torso stacked up as you resist those instinctive contortions. Drip enough water on the rock, and your body will start to believe that 'leaning up the mountain' is not the solution it appears to be. But you will need to develop your strength and perceptions over some considerable time as you progressively learn to keep up with the horse first in a leg-yield in walk, and then in trot.

When you ride a leg-yield parallel to the long side of the arena, I recommend riding the movement with the horse as straight as you can. Why turn his head away from the direction of motion when all you then do is encourage him to fall on his leading shoulder? If you dream of riding half-pass (which bends the horse towards the direction of motion) you are making this future set-up more difficult for yourself. So imagine that you begin riding a diagonal as normal, and are pointing your 'skis' straight towards the opposite quarter marker. Then, to initiate a leg-yield, you have to turn them so they are parallel to the long side of the arena. This requires the seat bone you are moving the horse away from

**Photo 10.9**
Denise rides half-pass in trot on the right rein. The box of her torso still looks well stacked, and the reach across of Piper's left hind and right fore is very clear.

to come back (think of our exercise with the stick, **Fig. 10.1**). Then, you have the challenge of keeping the horse in this position when he would much prefer to walk straight along the diagonal! So the question is, does he 'twizzle' you, so that you both revert to facing in that direction, or do you 'twizzle' him so that you both keep facing the short end of the arena? To succeed in this, you have to influence not just the part of the horse you are sitting on, but the whole horse from end to end. This is why the idea of skis can be so helpful.

As I have already said, the difficulty of stabilising yourself on the side/side plane is significantly increased by the dynamics of half-pass. Add that bend towards the direction of motion, and like Page in **Photo 9.8**, page 149, you could find yourself leaning up the mountain and consumed by those old contortions! In **Photo 10.9** we see Denise from the back, riding trot half-pass on the right rein. You can see how Piper's outside hind leg is crossing in front of the inside hind leg, and how the inside foreleg is stepping away from his midline. Denise has kept her vertical alignment well, and both sides of her torso are well stuffed. But the limitation here is that Piper does not have much bend, and it is the challenge of riding half-pass (as opposed to leg-yield) that Denise is finding difficult. She finds it easier in walk, where the forces acting on her body are smaller and it takes less muscle power to stabilise herself and have the influence she seeks.

Denise probably has a little more bend in **Photo 10.10**, where she is coming towards us in trot on the left rein. **Photo 10.11** shows half-pass in canter right, and you can see Piper's leading foreleg extending away from his midline. Al-

**Photo 10.10**
Denise trots towards the camera in half-pass left. The step looks powerful, but Piper does not have much bend. You can see that her outside leg is back, matching the way that her outside seat bone is back. She has kept her torso stacked much more effectively than Page in Photo 9.8 (page 149).

**Photo 10.11**
In canter half-pass to the right Piper shows some reach across with his leading foreleg, and a slight bend, but Denise is struggling not to have him 'twizzle' them both into the position where he canters straight across the diagonal.

though many people find canter easier (which makes sense as the horse is already moving on a diagonal from his outside hind leg to his leading inside foreleg), Denise is struggling more, and is barely stopping him from 'twizzling' her so that he gives himself the easier task of cantering straight along the diagonal.

Denise's lesson focused particularly on the way her left side could not be allowed to bulge out to the side as it does if her right side makes the creases we see in **Photo 10.4**. As it began, she told me how thinking about this had been helping her to stuff and stack both sides of her torso. This little adjustment had become the focus of the 'got it/lost it' game she had been playing with her horse, and it changed the way she could position Piper underneath her. Thus we continued to use that trigger, and I did not attempt to over-ride her discovery by introducing another. Shoulder-in right is more challenging for her than shoulder-in left, since the 'uphill' side (that she is moving away from) is also the side of her torso that tends to crease. If she leans to the right her left side begins to bulge, and conversely if she can stop it from bulging she can stop herself from leaning right. Half-pass to the left challenges her more than half-pass right, again by putting the 'uphill' side on the side she would tend to lean towards.

Remember my estimate that the instincts and forces that would deform her are ten times larger in half-pass than they are in leg-yield or shoulder-in, so it is no surprise that this is her weakest movement. Her 'lost its' have much more significance in half-pass than they do in any other movement, where they will reduce the quality of the movement, but not stop it from happening. But in her discovery about her left side, Denise was on the track of the next layer of skill that will help her to 'nail' half-pass. Already, her 'got its' are functioning at a level pretty deep within the onion, representing a level of skill that few people reach; but for some significantly more powerful 'got its' we must go to the next chapter, and see the Maestro at work!

# CHAPTER 11

# Advanced work: half-pass, piaffe, passage and pirouettes | Heather

As we look again at Heather, who is now riding Arabella, let us turn our attention back to the up/down plane, and the issues of sitting the trot. **Photos 11.1** and **11.2** show not trot but passage, which is a slow-motion trot performed in only the top three grades of dressage competitions (Grand Prix, Grand Prix Special, and Intermediare 2). They are taken within seconds of each other, but are not consecutive steps. To realise just how much up/down there is in passage, notice how Arabella's stomach is positioned relative to the bottom of the mirror in each photograph. Realise too that in **Photo 11.2** she has not yet reached the top of the 'up', and interestingly, her left hind leg has left the ground before her right foreleg. However, I have never seen this discrepancy with the naked eye. In collected work the horse's front legs work much harder than most people imagine, and researcher Dr Hilary Clayton has discovered that they proactively push the forehand up off the ground.

The way that Heather has absorbed this amount of up/down shows us the strategy by which ordinary riders can absorb the up/down of the trot, and the big difference between the two photographs lies in the angle of Heather's torso. On the 'up' she is leaning back, and on the 'down' she is a fraction ahead of vertical. Dr Clayton has also studied the biomechanics of skilled riders, and in trot the angle of the rider's torso has consistently varied by seven degrees. Given the dramatic up/down of passage we might expect a larger change than this, but my measurements make it less if anything. With my naked eye I have rarely seen Heather leaning back, and I was surprised to see her slightly behind vertical in all the photographs of the 'up'. But what the photographs really show us is that it is not the middle of her back that is changing on the up/down, it is the *angle of her hip joint*. So if you have been perfecting your 'wiggle in the middle' as you attempt to 'be supple and go with the movement', realise that you are using a different strategy to the world's most skilled and effective riders.

In Chapter 2 **Fig. 2.5** (page 43) shows how you can sit on a gym ball and mimic the mechanism of sitting trot, opening the angle between your thigh

**Photos 11.1–11.2**
These show the 'down' and the 'up' of passage, with Arabella's stomach and Heather's head moving through a remarkable range of motion (as shown by their position relative to the mirror). On the 'up' Heather's torso is inclined slightly back, whilst on the 'down' she is a fraction ahead of vertical. The mid-section of her back remains stable and unmoving, and only the angles of her joints have changed.

**Photo 11.3**
Arabella is showing beautiful form in piaffe. She is very stuffed, and uphill as she lowers her quarters and arches her neck into the rein. Heather's thigh is very out in front of her as she 'holds up the tea tray'.

and torso on the 'up', while leaning slightly back and taking more weight on your thighs. Then on the 'down' you close that angle again. This means that sitting trot is rather like a miniature version of rising trot, except that the angles between the thigh and torso are different. On the 'down' you are inclined slightly forward in rising trot and are vertical in sitting trot, while on the 'up' you are vertical in rising trot and slightly behind it in sitting. The knee will also open and close a little while sitting, but realise that the only movement is in the joints. The parts of the body between the joints must remain stable, and if you are not firmly stuffed in the area between your ribs and your hips, you will struggle to stop that wiggle.

Firstly, think of pulling your ribs down towards your hips, so that your torso remains short, with those elastic cords front and back staying the same length. Then try increasing the power of your bear down at this level by repeatedly making the sound 'sssh, sssh, sssh'. Make sure that you push into your back as well as your front. Also, increase the push into your sides, keeping firmly stuffed between the boards and the edge of your box even as you breathe out. Yes, skilled riders really are keeping their insides under this much pressure, and they have learned to sit comfortably with this feeling. It is like the smell they do not notice any more. But I expect you find it hard to tolerate – and perhaps you still do not believe me when I tell you that it takes this much pressure in your insides, coupled with this much muscle-power, for you to look as if you are sitting on your horse and doing nothing! The bottom line is that this high pressure stops skilled riders from wiggling; it gives them a much firmer, more imposing presence, and the diaphragm plays a big role in this. It attaches all around the inside of your ribcage, just above your bottom rib, acting as a cross membrane within your box (chemistry flask, page 62). Think of it joining your back and your front like the cross-bar in an 'H', holding the vertical lines apart and still. If that cross-bar can be distorted and wiggled by the horse's movement, so can the rest of you!

**Photo 11.3** shows piaffe, the trot-on-the-spot (or moving slightly forward) that again is seen only in the most advanced competitions. Heather is beautifully lined up with a light contact on the rein, and Arabella is showing very good form, with the quarters lowered, a good reach into the rein, and her feet lifted to just the right level. Riders who are struggling with this movement tend to start jiggling or shoving their seat around, but when the rider is well positioned she remains very still, as if sitting on the still centre of the moving horse. You might criticise Heather for having her heel up; but this is a drop in the ocean compared with the magnitude of all that she is doing right!

To return to our theme of the lateral movements, look at Heather in P**hotos 11.4** and **11.5**, riding shoulder-in left. **Photo 11.5** shows a very interesting moment when Arabella's right hindquarter is lowered as the hind leg on that side steps forward. The left hindquarter has passed its highest point, which it reached in the mid-stance phase of the stride when the cannon bone was vertical. This raising and lowering of each hindquarter is a natural feature of each step, which is perhaps exaggerated by the position of shoulder-in. Realise that despite the slope of Arabella's croup, Heather's pelvis and shoulders have remained level.

**Photo 11.4**
Arabella comes towards the camera in shoulder-in left. Notice that her nose is to the left of the centre of her chest: she is on four tracks, and bent to the inside with no hint of a jack-knife. Heather's torso is perpendicular to the part of Arabella's spine that she is sitting on, and her outside leg is back. You cannot tell from the shape of her 'box' that her outside seat bone position has advanced.

**Photo 11.5**
As Arabella advances her right hind leg that hindquarter lowers. But Heather's pelvis, torso, and shoulders have remained level. The vast majority of riders lose control of the seat bone in the direction of motion as this happens.

**Fig. 11.1**
From above, we see the horse's and rider's position in shoulder-in, renvers, travers and half-pass.

(a) In shoulder-in the rider's shoulders and pelvis are perpendicular to the horse's spine, with her outside leg back. Her seat bones are in the five to five position. The bend is to the opposite side to the direction of motion, which creates two conflicting demands. So the lower leg is back on the side that the seat bone is advanced.

(b) In renvers the horse is bent towards the direction of motion. The rider's pelvis and shoulders still look perpendicular to his spine, and her outside leg is back. Her seat bones are now in the five to five position. The lower leg that is back matches the seat bone that is back.

(c) In travers the horse is again bent towards the direction of motion. The rider's pelvis and shoulders still look perpendicular to his spine, but her seat bones are in the five past seven position. The lower leg that is back matches the seat bone that is back.

(d) Half-pass is just like travers, with an imaginary wall along the diagonal on the arena. As in (c) the horse is bent towards the direction of motion. The rider's seat bones are in the five past seven position. The lower leg that is back matches the seat bone that is back.

Transitions between shoulder-in and renvers, or shoulder-in and half-pass, require the rider to reverse the position of her seat bones. However, she can move between travers and shoulder-in without reversing them.

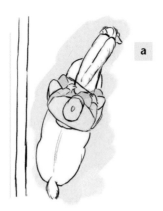

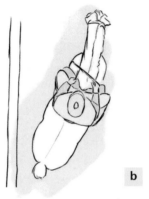

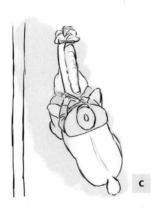

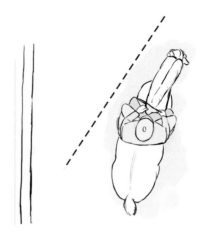

The angle between Heather's thigh and torso is more open on the right than it is on the left, and this is in response to the swing of the horse's ribcage to the left. This, too, is a natural feature of each step, for it positions the ribcage over the weight-bearing left hind, and makes space for the other hind leg to step forward. (Watch cats or dogs moving from the back, and you will see the same effect.) However, you can imagine how easily this change in the thigh/torso angle could further encourage Heather's right seat bone to slip away from the midline of the horse; but she is able to keep it close to the horse's spine, where the back remains most level. While Heather has 'side-stepped down the mountain' in perfect control of her body and her 'skis', you can see how easily her right side and the horse's right side could have slipped away from her.

**Photo 11.4**, where Arabella comes towards us, shows a similar moment in the stride, and we more clearly see the bend in her body. This puts her nose slightly to the left of the midline of her chest; but we can also clearly see that she has not jack-knifed at the wither – she has far too much stuffing for it to act as a hinge. Both horse and rider have their central axes vertical, and Arabella's shoulders are at about a 30° angle to the wall, as are Heather's shoulders and hips. Heather has turned the 'box' of her torso without any distortions, and by doing this she has 'turned the skis'. Also, she has turned them from the back, and she has *bent* them too. She has done this not only by stuffing and stacking the front leading edge of her box, but also by thinking of the edges of her box being curved in just the way that she wants to curve her horse.

Shoulder-in presents an anomaly, in that the horse is bent away from the direction of motion. The other lateral movements that include a bend (i.e. travers,

11.6

11.7

**Photo 11.6**
In shoulder-in right Arabella is leaning to the inside more than she is bending to the inside. Heather's lower leg and torso position look good, but she has lost her correct connection with one or both 'skis'.

**Photo 11.7**
As we look from the back at this point in the stride it is clear that Arabella's hind legs are positioned parallel to the track whilst her forehand has been moved to the inside. Heather has a few creases under her right armpit, and her head is slightly to the right. This is the first time her asymmetry has become visible.

renvers and half-pass) position the horse towards the direction of motion, so he is going – and bending – in the same direction. (See **Fig. 11.1**) The seat bone that is back is on the same side as the leg that is back, and there is no inherent contradiction. But shoulder-in requires one set of aids to position the horse, and a contradictory set to bend him. By the theory of skis and seat bones, the rider brings the horse's shoulders away from the wall by advancing her outside seat bone (in the direction of motion). But concurrently her outside leg should remain behind the girth to control the horse's hindquarters, and stop them from falling out.

Yet in **Photo 11.4** Heather has clearly met those conflicting demands – with her outside leg behind her inside leg, and her seat bones on the five past seven axis. If her seat bones and torso had remained facing straight down the long side, Arabella would have continued on two tracks as normal. If her 'box' had deformed in any way she would have paid the price with some distortion in Arabella's positioning. If her outside leg had come forward with her seat bone, the movement might have degenerated into a leg-yield, and become a less powerful gymnastic.

**Photo 11.6** shows the inside hind leg and the outside foreleg advancing as Arabella comes towards us in shoulder-in right, and again Heather's hips and pelvis are level, with her spine vertical. Arabella has less bend than she did on the left rein – in fact she appears to be leaning slightly right instead of bending right – making the movement technically less correct. **Photo 11.7**, taken from the back, shows us a moment close to the point when one pair of legs are just leaving the ground and the other pair are reaching it. This view of the hind feet makes it clear that they are travelling parallel to the wall even though the shoulders are on the inside track. Arabella's outside hindquarter is slightly lower than her inside hindquarter; but as ever, Heather's pelvis is unaffected by this. She just might, however, have a few more creases under her right armpit than under her left, with her right shoulder slightly lower than her left and her head slightly to the right – a miniature version of the asymmetry we have seen in both Sue and Denise (**Photo 7.6,** page 119, and **Photo 10.4,** page 154). From working with Heather over many years I know that her right side is not quite so easily stuffed, stacked or stabilised as her left. But it is a minimal difference compared to most riders, and not enough for her to lose control of that leading ski, and the horse's shoulders or quarters.

Looking at these photographs does not begin to show you just what it takes to ride shoulder-in with no distortions in your box, so your hips and shoulders are level and your spine vertical. To you, they are unlikely to infer great core muscle strength and stability, but this is what they are, in fact, showing us. Only this enables the rider to be so well in control of herself, and so precise in her riding. It is a far, far cry from the strength of kick and pull.

To put this strength in context, remember that in Chapter 10 on Denise, I suggested that it takes ten times as much stability for the rider to withstand the forces acting in leg-yield or shoulder-in (and to side-step down the mountain) as it does to withstand the forces that act on a circle. So let me rate the average rider's body control and stability on a nought to ten scale. Sadly, many riders are below a five, which suggests that they are more likely to hinder than help their horses. I say this not to discourage you – and I hope you are actually encouraged by reading this book and discovering that riding, and 'feel', are skills you can learn. On the contrary, I am using this scale to help me explain blue to the blind man, and to define exactly why it is that looking at the pictures and reading about the aids does not enable you to ride the movements well. Just as in the lesson with Millie, I am facing the problem of explaining that hidden dimension of riding – the role of muscle tone in creating stability.

So if I am to rate Heather's stability in shoulder-in, I must now use a scale that goes up to one hundred. If Heather's organisation rates as ninety-five (we all need some room for improvement!) then Denise and Page would rate in the sixties. Remember that they are being *ten times as effective* as the folks who are struggling on a circle. This is not to say that Page, Denise (or even Heather) always have their circles perfectly organised, but realise how taking these skills back to the circle makes the rider far more effective. Many riders can aspire to this skill level, although it takes the tenaciousness to make those ten thousand repetitions of each new co-ordination, and to pay attention in each successive moment. However, that *extra thirty to forty per cent* makes it possible for Heather to ride shoulder-in with the power that is required to place well in top-class competitions. Most of our horses shuffle along by comparison, reflecting our limp bodies and our 'all over the place' pelvises, seat bones and spines – not to mention our disorganised hands and legs.

Within the conventions of the wordscape, the aids for the lateral movements are described in terms of 'this hand here and that leg there', as if this were sufficient information to make the movements happen. This is only true if you are supremely talented, and I believe that these descriptions fail the vast majority of riders. In fact, I think they are so far from reality that they are little short of a joke. So if they do not work for you, it is not you that is failing (as our traditional culture would have you believe). Without the kind of core muscle strength that stabilises your 'box' you will struggle to come up with a semblance of a correct lateral movement. Even if you have a trainer who rides your horse on most days and fits him into the shape made by *her* correct box, it will not take him long to react to the difference between you and her.

The paradox within our culture is that those who were born with high isometric muscle strength (predominantly men) are so immersed in this hidden dimension of riding that they are like the goldfish who would never discover water. Nowhere in their description of riding is there any mention of high tone and the need for torso stability. Meanwhile, most riders never find that tone,

**Photo 11.8**
In half-pass left Arabella shows a clear bend to the left, and a huge range of motion as she abducts her left foreleg. Heather's right shoulder looks slightly dropped – she may again have creases under her right armpit.

171

**Photo 11.9**
In half-pass right we now see how much range of motion Arabella has in each of her limbs! She is bent less than she was in Photo 11.8.

11.10

11.11

**Photos 11.10–11.11**
These show moments in half-pass left and right that are almost mirror images. In Photo 11.10 Arabella's right hindquarter is dropped more than her left hindquarter in Photo 11.11, but in each case Heather's pelvis has remained level. There are some creases under her right armpit in Photo 11.11.

and do not enter that hidden dimension. Or they may read my work and be so shocked by the demands of bearing down and breathing that they fall at the first hurdle, and never discover just how much pay-off they will get for their efforts. Unless you were born with exceptional talent, learning to ride well is a journey into that hidden dimension. By peeling away those layers of the onion you progressively discover the ways in which finding more tone and more precision enables you to feel and organise your body so that you can feel and organise your horse.

The next set of photographs show half-pass, and as we look at these, we need to be thinking of a scale that goes to *one thousand*. (Heather, however, is one rider in a million in the way she can ride these!) Arabella, too, has great talent for this work, with a tremendous range of movement as she reaches each leg both away from the midline (known as abduction) and towards it (known as adduction). **Photo 11.8** shows just how far Arabella can abduct her left foreleg to the left – compare it with Piper in **Photos 10.9** and **10.10** (page 162). Notice too how much bend Arabella has to the left, and how her left hind crosses in front of her right hind. In **Photo 11.9** (shown opposite) she is coming towards us in half-pass right, showing the opposite phase in the stride where the inside hind leg is reaching over to the side, and the outside foreleg is crossing in front of the inside foreleg. The reach of the hind leg is so extreme that you might assume that her quarters must be leading (i.e. moving across the diagonal of the arena in advance of her right shoulder), but they are not. In these photographs we would have to rate Heather in the high 900s, where Page in **Photo 9.8** (page 149) would score 300, and Denise in **Photo 10.10** (page 162) would score about 450. Heather's talent is not just that she is not distorted by the sideways forces of the movement; it is that she can instigate those large forces, staying with them and organising them, so that she makes a correct and flamboyant movement that she has not restricted in any way.

In **Photo 11.10** Heather is riding away from us on the left rein, again with her pelvis and shoulders level, and her spine vertical. Arabella is showing a clear bend left, and a definite reach across of the right hind and left fore. The angle between the outside of Heather's thigh and her torso are again not the same on each side, and we have a lowered right hindquarter. **Photo 11.10** pretty much mirrors this moment in half-pass right, but here we see more level hindquarters, and some creases under Heather's right armpit. I still maintain that most riders will lean away from the direction of motion in half-pass as well as shoulder-in (like Page in **Photo 9.8**), so Heather is breaking my rule by showing the same distortion in her box that we saw in shoulder-in right (**Photo 11.7**). We will have to bring down her score by 50 points!

While Heather has not quite stuffed and stacked her right third, she has still done a very good job in this next layer of the onion, where 'nailing' half-pass requires her to become ten times as effective. It is now much more tempting to 'lean up the mountain', and far harder to keep up with the horse. Again it helps to think of being reeled in, and/or of a re-bar in the leading front edge of the box, which must be stacked in the right vertical relation to the horse's leading foreleg. The outer edges of Heather's box form firm boundaries that position the outer edges of Arabella's long back muscles underneath them. This takes enormous strength in the muscles that wrap around the torso. Additionally, Heather curves her edges in the way that she wants to curve her horse, and reinforces that shape through the way that she stuffs those outer thirds of her torso. All of these measures stop the horse from distorting the movement by not filling out enough on one side, while pushing out against her on the other. Taking these firm edges back into turns, circles and bends adds significantly to Heather's steering-power, making her even more precise, and leaving the horse with very few options for copping out!

The main theme of our lesson was the search for more definition in these outer edges, and we were also seeking ways to improve the reach in Arabella's topline. This small remaining aberration in Heather's right side is impacting on her horse, even though the half-pass looks spectacular. Changing this may well become 'the difference that makes the difference' in Heather's next break-through – creating the 'Aha!' moment that reorganises her body, and (yet again) reorganises the horse under her. Denise was glimpsing the power of defining those edges in her discovery that she must not let her left side bulge, and the differential between Heather's skill and that of Page and Denise really concerns the outer edges of the box. Without this extra precision the rider can make a decent stab at leg-yield and shoulder-in, but half-pass will always be rather hit-and-miss. Also, it will lack power.

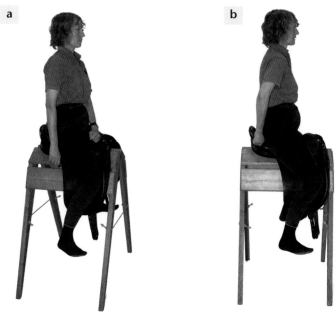

**Fig. 11.2**
(a) Putting your fist across the pommel and pushing your little finger against it can help you increase the strength in the outer edges of your box, as can pressure against the side of the saddle using the hand position in (b).

So if you feel you are making progress with shoulder-in but struggling in half-pass, it might help to think of your *sides* being held together by a bolt that passes right through you at the level of your diaphragm. This makes your diaphragm act like the cross-bar of an 'H' which now has your *sides* as its vertical lines. For a more powerful illustration of the resilience needed, imagine your sides like the sides of a squash racquet court. The impulse of the lateral movement is like a ball bouncing backwards and forwards between those walls. The walls must not dampen the force of the ball as it hits them, and reduce its 'bounce'. Equally, the impulse of the ball must not deform the walls. In many riders it would – or the ball might bounce with much less force within a much narrower area, as if the rider did not really exist all the way out to those firmly defined boundaries. The horse's legs would also move with much less force in a much narrower area, making the more average amount of movement that we saw with Piper and Promeso.

To increase the tone and awareness of those outer edges, and to make your stuffing push firmly up against them, stand close to a wall, extend your arm out sideways at shoulder height, and push your fist against that wall. As you ride, try making a fist out of one hand, and putting it across the pommel, so you can push against its side with the outside of your hand and little finger. Notice where your torso firms up in response. Then try pressing your thumb and first finger against the side of the saddle by your backside, and again, notice where you firm up in response. (See **Fig. 11.2**) Firming up both sides of the box also has a mental component, for you have to be able to perceive *both sides of your body at once*. But most riders pay attention to one side and stop noticing the other. Changing this is a strain on the brain, but without exceptional brainpower you cannot 'hold yourself together'.

We have now reached the point at which our story comes full circle. The initial chapter on Heather told the story of her first lesson, and how she had to take her stirrups up three holes and stop growing tall. We have also watched Jo and Diane become shorter as I stopped them from pulling their ribs up away from their hips, and losing the posture of a martial artist. The vast majority of riders start their lessons with me by discovering how much they gain from growing short, and from this beginning it can take quite some time for their riding to pass through the stages shown in this book.

By the time you reach the level of sophistication where you can attempt to line up the outer edges of your box over the outer edges of the horse's long back muscles, you have become unusually good at staying 'with' the horse as you 'side-step down the mountain'. So you are riding the lateral movements accurately and powerfully. But this can only happen after you have found both seat bones, mastered fencing-lunge position on the circle, got both boards on, and learned to stuff and stack both outer thirds. These are the skills that enable you to steer, 'turning like a bus' and maintaining the width and levelness of the horse's long back muscles. Work on circles will test and refine those skills admirably, preparing you for the ten-fold increase that is the challenge of the easier lateral movements!

These skills, in their turn, were built on the skills of elongating the horse into the rein by making length in the muscles of his back and neck, and drawing his back up under you. And *these* skills were built on the skills of a correct rising-trot mechanism, and the ability to sit in neutral spine while keeping weight down through the thigh. Prior to this, it all started by learning to bear down while breathing – a skill that brings with it the realisation that the primary challenge of riding is to match the forces of the horse's movement in every step he takes (be it on a straight line, a circle, or laterally). At the same time it also begins to dawn on you that the challenge involves being so in control of your own body that you can use it to rearrange the horse's body under you.

In moving through these stages you have learned a huge amount about your body. You have firmed up its soggy bits, filled in its empty bits, stilled its wiggly bits, let go of its tight bits, unravelled its twisted bits, defined its edges, and reached deep into the core of yourself, strengthening the deep muscles that everything else hangs from. In peeling away those layers you have gone from symptoms – which show in the extremities and edges – right into the core, where you find the deep-rooted causes of problems that most people presume are superficial. So like Denise, you might find that your wiggling lower legs become more still as you learn to stuff and stack both outer thirds, and extend that stuffing down into your legs.

In making this journey, you have also faced some of your demons. They might be performance anxiety, fear, the inability to set goals, the inability to focus, the tendency to over-focus and try too hard, or the desire to get it all right *now*! Through overcoming all of these hurdles, it could even be said that you have become more intelligent, for if intelligence is defined as 'the ability to respond' you can now respond to your horse on a subtle level that you could not even have dreamt about at the beginning. You have even gained the mental skill to remain 'in the moment' to the same degree as your horse! You can play the 'got it/lost it' game with him in a way that earns you his respect – and perhaps the respect of the world. And as we all know, neither of these are given lightly.

Then, when you finally become able to firm up the edges of the box and position the horse underneath them, you discover a curious fact. If you line up on one side, you find yourself falling off the edge of the long back muscle on the other side, as if your torso were too wide. And then if you line up on that side, you fall off the first side… and so this goes on, in a game of 'ping-pong' that is reminiscent of the challenge of getting both boards on (see page 130). There is only one answer, and that is to find a way of *narrowing the whole torso* so that both sides of it fit over those edges (hence the idea of the bolt that holds them together). And guess what you find then? Just like a liquid that has been poured into a narrower container, your torso suddenly feels taller.

As this happens, your legs might begin to feel *longer*, for the narrowing of your box creates firmness and 'connection' in the muscle chain that runs from beneath the armpit, down the sides of the ribcage and pelvis, and down the outside of the thigh and calf to the foot. I call this the chain of 'externals'. The boards might start to feel longer too, and they start to form part of a muscle chain which continues into inner thigh and calf, down to the inside of the foot – the chain I call 'internals'. Given that any chain is only as strong as its weakest link, one tiny disconnection will render the whole chain dysfunctional. But once these muscle chains do connect you can more clearly feel the stuffing that lies in between them, and this can really make your wobbly legs firm up – as I have promised Denise. Then, it begins to make sense that you might 'step into the inside stirrup' on a circle, or step into the stirrup in the direction of a lateral movement. For you would respond to those words by *firming up those muscle chains and the stuffing that lies in between them*. If you are not one of the very few gifted riders in whom they already function well (on both sides), you will hear those words, push into the stirrup and lift your seat bone – which gets you into big trouble.

In Chapter 1 on learning I suggested that since our traditional tenets of riding came out of the mouths of the world's great riders, they must represent the tip of their iceberg of skill – the part of it that reached up into in their conscious mind, allowing them to talk about it (see **Fig. 1.2**, page 23). Meanwhile, its vast base remained submerged in the unconscious, as the instinctive 'know-how' that is inaccessible to language. So it makes perfect sense that our traditional sayings must be the XYZs of riding – the discoveries that are made through time and talent – and not its ABCs. But since they are presented to us as beginning points rather than end points, they become enormously confusing. Who would think that 'grow up tall' could mean anything other than 'lift your ribs up away from your hips'?

To return to our photographs, **Photos 11.12** and **11.13** (both shown overleaf) show canter pirouettes to the right and left. **Photo 11.12** really shows how much Arabella's croup has lowered, and **Photo 11.13** shows the bend most

**Photo 11.12**
In this canter pirouette to the right, Arabella has really lowered her croup, and her inside hind leg has come to the ground before her outside foreleg, breaking that diagonal pair. Heather's upper body is inclined slightly forward. She has her 'front tendons up' and is 'holding up the tea tray' as she keeps Arabella's forehand lifting in each stride.

**Photo 11.13**
In this pirouette to the left, we see how Heather's outside shoulder is back, as she keeps fencing lunge position. Her outside leg and outside seat bone are also back, with her seat bones in the five to five position.

clearly. In both photographs the inside foreleg is in the air, and in **Photo 11.12** only the toe of the outside foreleg is on the ground. The inside hind leg has come down before it, breaking that diagonal pair. Dr Hilary Clayton's research at Michigan State University has shown that this always happens in a canter pirouette, even if the discrepancy cannot be seen with the naked eye. Notice how Heather is leant slightly forward in this phase of the stride. Her thigh is rather horizontal, and this is part of how she keeps the front of the horse lifting in each stride. Like Diane and Denise, Heather keeps her front tendons up, and keeps 'holding up the tea tray', lifting Arabella's forehand and creating this extreme of collection. Her strategy is such a far cry from leaning back, which most people assume must weight the hindquarters (a fallacy we exposed on page 100 and in **Fig. 6.2**). Notice how Heather still has that perfect straight line from her hand to her elbow to the horse's mouth, with a quiet hand that does not pull.

As we look from the front in **Photo 11.13** we can see how Heather's and Arabella's axes are aligned. Also, we can see that Heather's outside shoulder is back, just as it would be on a circle. She is again in fencing-lunge position, making a strong wall with her outside aids. She has her outside seat bone and board to push the horse around from, and her inside board to receive her. Her chin is over the horse's mane. She is stuffed and stacked in both outer thirds, keeping width and stuffing in both of the horse's long back muscles. She can create and contain that width with the strong boundaries of her box. Not much to ask, especially while maintaining the jump and the tempo of the canter and turning the forehand around the quarters!

But she is doing something else too. My description above only talks about how she is influencing the part of the horse that is directly under her; but in reality she is influencing the length of horse that is in front of her, and the length of horse that is behind her, turning and organising those skis. My favourite way of describing that influence compares the rider's torso to a mast that has guy wires extending both forward and back. Think of a suspension bridge that has one pier at its centre and has the roadway hung from its wires: bizarre as it may sound, the horse's topline can (in effect) be hung from the rider's torso in a similar way. The wires originate both from the boards and from the edges of the box, and they connect to specific parts of the horse. (See **Fig. 11.3** overleaf) They give the rider a croup-to-ears influence on both sides of him, and while they might be figments of my imagination they really can help you – and they have helped Heather – to stay aligned, and to avoid distortions. In fact, our most recent breakthrough (eighteen months after these photographs were taken) has involved some reorganisation of the wires that extend from the back of Heather's right board and organise the horse's right hindquarter.

I think this idea of the mast is the ultimate image – the best description I can find to explain the influence of the world's most gifted riders. This extends from top to toe, poll to tail, board to board, edge to edge, and top line to underline. It 'tunes' both horse and rider in a resonance that links tonal quality with tonal

**Fig. 11.3**

The rider's torso is like a mast, with wires connecting forward and back from the lines of the boards, and from the edges of the box. The horse also has boards and edges to his box, which, when he is going straight (and even around a corner), should be lined up in front of and behind the rider's boards and edges. The three wires from specific points on the rider's boards connect to specific points just to the side of the horse's spine and crest. The three connections from the edges of her box connect to the outside edges of these muscle chains.

(a) Shows the two sets of wires that extend from the rider's right board and edge. The distance between each pair is the width of the muscle chains that extend forward and back on the horse's neck and back. There would be similar connections from her left side to the left side of the horse.

(b–e) From above we can see how the distance between each pair of wires defines the edges of the muscle chains that extend forward and back on the horse. (e) Shows the top and middle sets of wires.

The ability to line up the horse under you, in front of you, and behind you, and to 'hang' him from these wires makes your riding supremely ethical, and effective. Very few riders in the world can do this in all gaits, and in all directions and movements, but – given enough time to progress through all of the stages in this book – it is potentially a learnable skill.

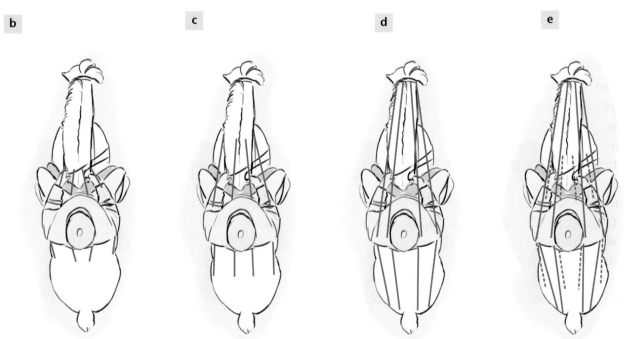

quality, brain with brain, and energy system with energy system. Perhaps it even links soul to soul. Few will achieve this at such a refined level as Heather – and some will rubbish the idea that such refinement exists or has value. But those of us who yearn for a sense of 'oneness' with our horses can experience it much more often than we might have imagined, for these wonderful experiences are available on each layer of the onion.

Magical rides do not require continued perfection, or the refinement of Grand Prix – they only require us to keep playing the 'got it/lost it' game, matching challenges with skills in each successive moment. The ultimate experiences happen whenever a new breakthrough adds another tool to our rider's toolkit, giving us a new way to solve an old problem, and moving us into a deeper layer of the onion. But whenever we have the skills and awareness to solve the challenges we perceive in our current layer, we can enjoy a very satisfying ride. There will, of course, be days when our horses are in a mental state that tries our patience, as well as days when they delight us by responding so well. And there will always be more challenges to come; but until they reveal themselves we can revel in our successes – as long as we do not fall into the trap of thinking that we have 'arrived'. It takes more than a modicum of discipline to keep remembering that we will have to bake that 'trot cake' all over again within each successive ride!

With practice we can actually train ourselves to reproduce the physical, mental and emotional aspects of satisfying, if not exceptional, rides. We do not have to pray to the gods to make them happen; instead they can grow and evolve from the (apparently) simple beginnings of lining up and bearing down. But within each of the layers of the onion, there will be times when the precision and the perception that our horses require are beyond our current resources. This may test our willingness to stick with it – but there is a lot to be said for continuing the search for new skills. Staying 'in the moment' definitely beats resorting to brute force and ignorance, or mindlessly riding round and round. For if we always do what we always did, we always get what we always got.

In my experience, few of life's adventures can yield such gifts as the adventure you can have with your horse. All we ever do is a few variations on the theme of walk, trot and canter, in straight lines, on turns and circles, and while going sideways. As we do this we travel both the outer terrain of the riding arena and the world, and the inner terrain of our being. It is changes in *perception* which make our sport so captivating, for even as years go by, they can continue to shed new light on the issues of riding – the oh-so-familiar stumbling blocks that frustrate so many of us. T. S. Elliot may never have ridden a dressage test but he really understood the nature of learning and change when he stated so beautifully in 'The Four Quartets': 'We shall never cease from exploration, and at the end of all our exploring we come back to the place where we started and see it as if for the first time.'

# Epilogue

IN WRITING THIS BOOK, I wanted to take the map that I have created of good riding skills to a level beyond my writing so far. I wanted to give an overview of skilled riding as I currently understand it, to include the lateral movements, and to help you understand how the phrases that you have heard so often might have a meaning (in the brainscape) that is different to the meaning you had assigned to them. I also wanted you to understand how easily this can happen in a culture that specialises in using 'woolly' language, and that routinely presents Xs as As.

I hope you will agree with me that presenting this more precise theory through the stories of the riders and their respective lessons makes it much more accessible, and brings it to life. But there is danger in taking the map as far as I have taken it, for the additional information is likely to tempt you to try to run before you walk – to attempt PQR before you have mastered ABC. I sometimes meet riders who tell me that they have been working on their boards (a PQR idea); but to my eye they have skipped over the basics that underlie it. Then, in our work together, we have to *back up* to those basics, and rebuild from there. So as you read my words and apply them to your riding, please be thorough. Go step by step, and be willing to take it slowly. You will be amply repaid for your tenacity.

Many people want riding skills to be much simpler and easier to learn than they actually are. (Blame the sensitivity of horses if you must; blame the laws of physics if you must; but do not blame me – I am just the map bearer!) This desire for easy accomplishment is understandable – and as I said at the start of this book, none of us can possibly know what challenges lie ahead of us when we first set foot in the stirrup. However, I despair sometimes when people seem to *want* the kind of traditional, simplistic explanations that, to my mind, do not hold water. So I hope I have instilled in you a desire to ask questions, and a quest for knowledge that will not be satisfied by platitudes.

Baron Blixen von Finecke, who won an Olympic gold medal in eventing, coached riding until he was in his eighties. He was a rather frail old man when he told a friend of mine: 'The problem with riding is that once you've worked out how to do it, you're so old that you can't do it any more.' Having a map like this one can speed up your learning process immensely. As Heather said in her foreword, it can save you from many dead-end roads and make the learning process much more captivating.

I wish you lots of fun as you begin to play the 'got it/lost it' game with your horse. I hope you enjoy it as much as I do – for as long as you keep putting your backside in the saddle, the game will never stop!

# Index